SCOTTISH MUSIC YEARBOOK

By Julia Read

Scottish Piper and Celtic Harpist

Contents

Introduction

January

  1 January: Auld Lang Syne
    Composer: Robert Burns – lyrics, traditional tune

  2 January: Space (Orchestral version)
    Composer: Biffy Clyro

  3 January: The Secret Wedding, Braveheart Theme
    Composer: James Horner

  4 January: Outlander Theme Season 1
    Traditional, arranged by Bear McCreary

  8 January: I Wish I Was in Glasgow
    Composer: Billy Connolly

  17 January: I'm On My Way
    Composer: The Proclaimers

  24 January: Silence
    Composer: The Monks of Iona

  25 January: A Man's a Man for A That
    Composer: Words – Robert Burns, Tune - traditional

February

  2 February: We Will Rock You
    Composer: Queen

  14 February: The Clumsy Lover
    Composer: Neil Dickie

  21 February: A Meditation on Iona
    Composer: Sir James MacMillan

  26 February: Love is an Arrow
    Composer: Aberfeldy

  27 February: Bells of Dunblane
    Composer: Pipe Major Robert Mathieson

March
 1 March: The Duke of Fife's Welcome to Deeside
    Composer: James Scott Skinner
 5 March: Sam the Skull
    Composer: Harry Hagan
 8 March: The Jeely Piece Song
    Composer: Adam McNaughton
 10 March: All the Bagpipe Tunes Ever
    Composer: Multiple composers
 26 March: Shang-a-Lang
    Composer: Bill Martin – lyrics, Phil Coulter - music
April
 1 April: Anno/Four Seasons: birds (spring)
    Composer: Anna Meredith MBE
 5 April: The Banjo Breakdown
    Composer: Pipe Major Donald MacLeod MBE
 7 April: Swerving for Bunnies
    Composer: Ailie Robertson
 9 April: Oft in the Stilly Night
    Composer: words Thomas Moore, music Sir John Stevenson
 16 April: Scotland the Brave
    Composer: Words – Cliff Hanley
 27 April: Moments in Time
    Composer: Dame Evelyn Glennie et al
May
 3 May: Looking at a Rainbow Through a Dirty Window
    Composer: Calum Stewart
 5 May: Farewell to Stromness
    Composer: Sir Peter Maxwell-Davies
 12 May: Solitary Citizen

Composer: Malcolm Lindsay

29 May: The Atholl Highlanders
Composer: Traditional

June

1 June: The Gael
Composer: Dougie MacLean

2 June: Caledonia
Composer: Dougie MacLean

3 June: The Braes o' Balquhidder
Composer: Robert Tannahill

4 June: Dignity
Composer: Deacon Blue (Ricky Ross)

7 June: Bruce's Last Breath
Composer: Paul Leonard-Morgan

8 June: The Legend of Wallace
Composer: Paul Leonard-Morgan

9 June: Dunad
Composer: Paul Leonard-Morgan

10 June: Mary Queen of Scots
Composer: Paul Leonard-Morgan

11 June: Ally's Tartan Army
Composer: Andy Cameron

12 June: Donald Where's Your Troosers
Composer: Neil Grant (Iain MacFayden) – music, Andy Stewart - words

13 June: Crags of Tumbledown Mountain
Composer: Pipe Major Jim Riddell

19 June: The False Bride
Composer: Unknown

21 June: Heartwood

Composer: Karine Polwart, Seckou Keita

  24 June: Highland Wedding
  Composer: Donald Cameron

July
  1 July: A Man's a Man for A That
  Composer: Words – Robert Burns, Tune - traditional

  3 July: She Moved Through the Fair
  Composer: Irish traditional

  4 July: The Last Rose of Summer
  Composer: Thomas Moore

  5 July: My Apartment
  Composer: The Humblebums

  6 July: Mary Skeffington
  Composer: Gerry Rafferty

  7 July: Stuck in the Middle with You
  Composer: Steelers Wheel

  8 July: Baker Street
  Composer: Gerry Rafferty

  10 July: Psalm 16: 8 – 9
  Composer: Gaelic psalm singers

  15 July: In a Big Country
  Composer: Big Country (Stuart Adamson)

  17 July: I'm Gonna Be (500 miles)
  Composer: Craig Reid, Charlie Reid

  23 July: Major Thomas of Cairnleith
  Composer: Lindsay Ross

  24 July: Wishing Well
  Composer: Angus MacPhail

  25 July: Margaret's Waltz
  Composer: Pat Shuldham-Shaw

26 July: Coilsfield House
   Composer: Nathaniel Gow
31 July: We Are stars
   Composer: Callum Beattie

August
   8 August: Cumha Mhic an Toisich (or Mackintosh's Lament)
      Composer: Piobaireachd - Ancient
   9 August: Cumha Mhic Shimidh (or Lord Lovat's Lament)
      Composer: Piobaireachd - Ancient
   12 August: Little Bird
      Composer: Annie Lennox
   18 August: Hearts of Olden Glory
      Composer: Rory Macdonald / Calum Macdonald
   19 August: The Bonnie Banks of Loch Lomond
      Composer: Traditional - unknown
   21 August: My Love She's But a Lassie Yet
      Composer: Words – Robert Burns, Tune - traditional
   23 August: A Girl Like You
      Composer: Edwyn Collins
   24 August: Waverley Steps
      Composer: Fish

September
   1 September: God Most High
      Composer: David Lyon
   20 September: Ali Bali Bee
      Composer: Robert Coltard
   22 September: An Old Friend
      Composer: Fergus McCreadie
   26 September: Downton Abbey Theme Music
      Composer: John Lunn

October
- 2 October: 故郷の空
  Composer: Lyrics – Robert Burns, Music - unknown
- 14 October: Wings
  Composer: William Newstead
- 27 October: Culloden Moor Suite: March
  Composer: Bobby Wellins
- 30 October: Assassins Creed III: any track
  Composer: Lorne Balfe

November
- 3 November: I Don't Wanna Fight
  Composer: Lulu
- 5 November: The Land of the Mountain and the Flood
  Composer: Hamish MacCunn
- 11 November: Flowers of the Forest
  Composer: Words – Jean Elliot
- 14 November: Fingal's Cave
  Composer: Felix Mendelssohn
- 15 November: Sea Plaint (Osnadh na Mara), Op. 14 No. 4
  Composer: Julian Nesbitt
- 27 November: You & I
  Composer: Alec Dalglish (Skerryvore)
- 30 November: Flower of Scotland
  Composer: Roy Williamson

December
- 3 December: Niel Gow's Lament to his Second Wife
  Composer: Niel Gow
- 9 December: Western Isles
  Composer: Peat and Diesel
- 10 December: Miss Drummond of Perth

Composer: Niel Gow
11 December: The Highland Brigade at Magersfontein
Composer: John MacLellan
14 December: Ae Fond Kiss
Composer: Words - Robert Burns
21 December: Amazing Grace
Composer: Words - John Newton
25 December: Precious
Composer: Annie Lennox
26 December: I Love a Lassie
Composer: Sir Harry Lauder
31 December: Let's Go Round Again
Composer: Average White Band

INTRODUCTION

Scotland is appreciated in many countries around the world. Sadly, we can't all visit, especially at the time of writing this book (2020/21) when the world is in global shutdown due to Covid. So, I decided that I would write a book of Scotland, its scenery, traditions, history for all those who love the place and are maybe unable to get themselves there in person. My personal take on this is to do it through the lens of Scottish music. Now Scottish music isn't all bagpipes and diddly diddly folk music. I hope that you know that already. But if you don't then let this book act as a little guide.

Throughout the year, on selected days, I will suggest a piece of music[1] that was composed by a Scot. There are a few exceptions, but I'll explain those when you get to them. For example if you take a glance at the table of contents you'll see that Queen has made it into the 2 February. This isn't a reference to the soundtrack that they recorded for the film Highlander. It is for a completely different reason – but you'll find that out when you get to February. Mostly though, the music that is recommended in this book is composed by Scottish musicians. I also make recommendations of artists that you can search out.

I hope that you will appreciate the music in this book, although I won't be getting all technical on you and expecting you to listen out for tone, pitch and volumes etc. Instead this is a book that appreciates the music and tells of Scotland through its music, in the form of story. The stories are sometimes of the composers and at other times they are of the scenery and history of Scotland told as an allegory of the music. As a bagpiper and celtic harpist, much of the music of Scotland has interweaved itself into my life and so the stories are sometimes mine. Elsewhere I am going to take you into the story and have you journey through time and space to experience a little piece of Scotland. My hope is that by dipping into this book throughout the year on the dates selected, you or the person that you gift this book to, will get to experience Scotland and explore it through its music. And we are talking all genres here: Jazz, TV scores, folk, rock, R&B, traditional, classical, pop, humour.

Why not dip into the month that you are in right now? Let's visit some of those Lochs and start tasting some whisky!

JANUARY

1 January: Auld Lang Syne

*Composer: Robert Burns –
lyrics, traditional tune*

When I think of Auld Lang Syne I am reminded of all the times that I have played it as a bagpiper, on the stroke of midnight on New Year's Eve. Arriving at the hotel where I've been booked to play I pull up into the car park at 11pm on a dark and often frosty December night. Driving past the function room and hearing the boom boom boom of the house band playing for the party that is in full swing and seeing the flashing coloured lights of the disco strobe. Parking up and getting out of the car, I'll open the back door where my bagpipes and the rest of my uniform lie. I take out the pipers plaid and wrap it around my body and drape it over shoulder, pinning it on with the cairngorm brooch that my mother used to use when she was a young lady piper in the 50s. Putting the Glengarry on my head, I check in the car window that the feather plume is straight. Then lifting my pipes up from the back seat – pre tuned I might add because there is no way to tune pipes up before a New Year's eve job at the actual event as it would give the game away that I'm there! Then I lock up my car and sneak in the back way to reception, making that sure the guests don't see me. We do the admin at hotel reception, confirming which function room I'm going to play in, paying up etc then I'll get secreted off to a hotel room. That is where I wait. For an hour, drinking a coffee, watching a bit of New Year's eve TV. I can hear the faint boom boom boom of the merry makers downstairs and I keep a very close eye on the clock – this is one of those jobs when timing is all important. I think of all the other pipers all around the UK at this exact time, waiting in the wings, waiting for midnight, just like I am, and there is a spirituality to that for me. I wish them all luck in my head and feel connected to them all somehow.

Five minutes before midnight I come out of my hidy place, head downstairs so that I can go to the reception room, hovering outside waiting for the DJ to countdown to midnight. 10 – 9 – 8 well you get the idea, right to 0 – happy New Year everyone! That's my cue - strike up the pipes and come in with Auld Lang Syne. The merrymakers link arms in a circle with me in the middle. I speed up and up and up. Two verses is enough, then I stop as abruptly as I started so that they can all wish each other a Happy New Year. Follow this up with a little 6/8 jig for a bit of dancing, then march out to Scotland the Brave and hopefully it will have given everyone an experience to remember of the fun night they had bringing in the New Year.

As I drive home I am less anxious than the drive there. That was tinged with the anxiousness of "will I get there on time, can't miss midnight, hope there are no traffic incidents". But driving home is more meditative. The deed is done. New Year has been brought in. All the Auld acquaintances have not been forgot and they have been firmly brought to mind. I drive home with thoughts of all those other pipers in the UK doing exactly the same thing at this exact same time. Of all the other pipers around the world, who have done exactly the same thing as their time zone passed midnight.

I suppose that that is what Auld Lang Syne signals to me; a night of connection. Connection for all the people at the party linking arms, dancing in a circle. Connection in spirit thinking of all the pipers, travelling the same path as me and driving home at 1am after another successful New Year's eve gig. As I write this we are coming out of 2020, the year of the covid pandemic. Being unable to meet up hasn't prevented us all connecting; there's been zoom, whats app, telephones, waving through windows. So here's to

Auld Lang Syne, to connections for the New Year, be they in mind, body or spirit.

Julia Read

2 January: Space (Orchestral version)

Composer: Biffy Clyro

A throw away remark on the TV program 'Only Connect' led me to look at Scottish rock group Biffy Clyro. Apparently, the band members of Biffy Clyro used to amuse themselves coming up with names of products that the singer Cliff Richard might merchandise. One of these imaginary products was 'Cliffy Biro', which would have images of Cliff's face placed all over the pen. So it was that cliffy biro morphed into Biffy Clyro and the name of the band was formed. My interest was piqued in this story by my desire to find Scottish music for this book and so I went exploring, and Space, the orchestral version is what I found. It is an amazing production and a collaboration between some extremely talented musicians. The lyrics of Space refer to knowing the truest meaning of love in its absence and of shared moments bringing joy. The final scenes of the Space video end with violinist's fingers going on and off the string so that we are aware now of a subtle wave of sound, leaving a ripple as the music finishes. I don't pretend to know what the song Space is about. I have read the lyrics a few times now and I can take several meanings from it. It could be about two people being apart or it could be about being apart from a particular place or it could be about being distanced from a relationship with a Higher Power. I am going to take this latter meaning because it fits with my experience of finding faith. I also think that it has some relevance for the second January. Let me explain.

The second January often marks a period of raw energy for those that have set a New Year's resolution and are setting at it with fervour. This raw energy is the first step toward a type of faith in my experience and it is fuelled by a desire for something – to lose weight, to get fit, to get financial freedom. If a specific goal has been set and it is attacked with a do or die willingness, much like a rugby tackle to a giant boulder, then this raw fuel can last long enough for faith to get in and take over. Faith that you can actually do this thing. That faith can then replace the raw fuel as an energy source. When you hit the cold bleak days of February and have to do that run that you had committed yourself to do, then hopefully you've got all those days from January, when you did go out running, to prove to yourself that you can do this. Faith grows. That is a faith in oneself. But the thing that I have come to experience is that there is another type of faith, a faith in something greater than myself and I hear echoes of that faith in the song Space. Its presence is like the ripple that is set up at the end of Space by the violinists. Soft, quiet, subtle, but persisting and always there if one knows what to listen for. It can be found in the joy that comes from sharing moments or rather being Aware of moments, Aware of the Space around us and everything that is in that Space. My life can be powerful without it, but it is more powerful with it; I have understood the truest meaning of love because it was absent from my life but is present now. This is how I interpret the song Space anyway. To me it is a song about finding faith in a power greater than myself. The intuition that is inside of me, guiding me, and which I have so often ignored in the past. That intuition used to give me sage advice like 'after this biscuit, that is the last one that I'm going to eat' but I so often ignored it. Following that intuition in each minute of each day has meant that I achieve my goals one day at a time, calmly and peacefully. I no longer have to push at them with the raw energy of a New Year's resolution.

Please forgive me if this all sounds condescending, I don't wish it to be. I am merely sharing from my own experience of faith. Whatever this New Year holds in store, at the very least faith in oneself seems like a darn good thing to tackle it with.

3 January: The Secret Wedding, Braveheart Theme

Composer: James Horner

If you are yet to return to work, why not round off the holiday period with a spot of afternoon movie watching. To introduce you into the mood of a bit of TV relaxation, my recommendation for today is Braveheart, or rather the theme from Braveheart entitled 'The Secret Wedding'. It was created by the prolific film composer James Horner. To my ears it is a piece that is incredibly evocative of Scotland. As the music swells I see the burgeoning Scottish rivers pushing through the peat meadows, then with a flurry and a run on the violins, the stream ripples and eddies around granite rocks. The quavering flute introduces the theme and whisps in and out of the music like the spirit of an ancient clansman. That is certainly what I hear and see when I listen to the original soundtrack as recorded by the London Symphony Orchestra. But, I can recommend another recording for you to search out. This is from an ensemble called 'Fordante'. An ensemble of violinist, viola, oboe and cello with arrangements by Phil Mountford. Theirs is a particularly beautiful performance, accompanied by a video full of images of Scottish Lochs, mist covered mountains, castles and Caledonian forests. The oboe in particular brings a haunting sound of times past and, to my ears anyway, makes a wonderful substitute to the flute from the original soundtrack.

4 January: Outlander Theme Season 1

Traditional, arranged by Bear McCreary

Whilst we are in the spirit of a bit of TV watching, after yesterday's entry, how about continuing the theme and going for the incredible arrangement of Skye Boat Song that Bear McCreary created for Season 1 of Outlander. In fact, all of his arrangements for all of the seasons are worth listening to. But I can only recommend one per day and as season 1 started off the introduction of Bear McCreary's work to a new audience we'll start here; it is also the most Celtic of the arrangements and hence the most relevant to be included in this book on Scottish music. This arrangement has everything Celtic in it. The pipes and drums of a Scottish pipe band, the hauntingly magical voice of a bonnie maiden (Raya Yarborough – ok, not Scottish, but we can imagine!), celtic fiddle motives, celtic flute and a last part accompaniment to the low rumble of canons sufficient to mark the narrative arc that the Outlander story takes. If you haven't watched Outlander yet, be prepared to hunker down for some box set binging as Claire and Jamie start their journey together with this music of Outlander season 1. Listen out for Bear McCreary's music, it is phenomenal.

8 January: I Wish I Was in Glasgow

Composer: Billy Connolly

Billy Connolly's off the wall, Glaswegian, working class humour is known the world over. Many an audience have been in stitches at his comedy stand up gigs and he is well known also for his humorous folk style music. But this little tune is not funny. Instead it is poignant and beautiful. In 'I Wish I Was in Glasgow', Billy sings about the Glasgow that created him into the man that he became. He writes with fondness about the town that he grew up in. A town which was at the time, as he puts it, in decline. It was a ship building town, an industrial town, yet Billy's song talks of a warmth, the warmth of friendships, even if it was a bit rough.

What I like about this song is the indomitable spirit of gratitude that pervades it. There is no significance to the date, 8 January. I just thought that a little dollop of gratitude at the start of the year might be a good thing. I hope that you enjoy Billy's song and find many things in your 8 January day to be grateful for.

17 January: I'm On My Way

Composer: The Proclaimers

You know those days that we often get in the middle of January? The skies are clear blue and the sun is streaming in through the window beckoning us outside for a good old walk in the crisp fresh winter air. Well, 'I'm On My Way' by The Proclaimers is a tune for just such a day. It is bouncy and fun and full of energy; perfect for getting the day off to a good mood start. It is also perfect for getting us into a Scottish mood because of the strong Scottish accents that characterises The Proclaimers' songs. Twin brothers Craig and Charlie Reid, both born in Leith Edinburgh, formed the rock duo in 1983. They had many hits, which I am sure that you are all acquainted with and if not then please please go and find their album 'Sunshine on Leith'.

So here's to a good old sunshiny wintery day and a fabulous joyous song. If you have stuck with your New Year's resolution so far, then put this song on and sing out loud "I'm on my way!".

Julia Read

24 January: Silence

Composer: The Monks of Iona

On 17 January I referred to those crisp sunny days that we often get in January. But let's face it, during this time of the year a lot of the Northern Hemisphere is cloaked in snow. Places such as Boston, Oslo and most certainly the Highlands of Scotland are often blanketed in that fluffy white stuff. If that is the case for you and you are currently gazing out on a snow fall drifting down from the skies above and covering up all that is around you, then you will be in a perfect situation to appreciate the Creation 'Silence' from the monks of Iona.

Iona is an island off an island off the West coast of Scotland; specifically, it is an island to the west of the Isle of Mull. The Monks of Iona occupied it during the Dark Ages and it is possible to go there now and visit their Abbey. In his excellent book 'Civilisation', Kenneth Clark says that of all the many times that he has visited Iona he has never gone there without the feeling that "some God is in this place". I definitely agree. When I was there, I had a strong feeling of all the prayers that those monks had said. To me it was like their prayers had formed the warp and weft of a large cloth that was then laid over the entire island and that they did this year after year, so that the island was covered in layers upon layers of these prayer cloths. Each of my footprints seemed to sink deeply into these prayer cloths that covered the place. Kenneth Clark describes how and why the monks were here at all. He talks of the chaos that came after the fall of the Roman/Greco empire and how this opened up a space for barbarians like the Huns to enter.

These turbulent events of the 6th Century forced a migration of the few protectors of Civilisation to the Atlantic, seeking inaccessible fringes such as the Hebrides and Iona. They sought security and stability to copy books and protect what they knew of Christianity and civilisation; and so, they came to Iona and made it their home.

You won't be able to go to your favourite streaming service and download this creation of 'Silence' that the Monks of Iona made. It is the sound of the place. I can help you hear it though. As that new covering of snow falls gently outside and dampens down the noise that us humans make, go outside and just be. That is the 'Silence' that the Monks of Iona created.

Julia Read

25 January: A Man's a Man for A That

Composer: Words – Robert Burns, Tune - traditional

It is the 25th January and that can only mean one thing. Yes, of course, it is Burns night. A night for celebrating all things Robert Burns. A night for putting on your kilt, an argyle or prince Charlie jacket and tucking a sgian dubh into your hose before heading out the door to a fabulous evening at your chosen Burns night venue. You can pretty much be guaranteed of finding a Burns night supper in every country on every continent of the world; so loved is this great Scottish tradition.

As a young fledgling piper, my first experiences of playing at a Burns night was as a member of a pipe band playing every year at the Returned Services Association (RSA) in Auckland, New Zealand. I remember being encouraged to be part of the playing in the haggis. On my very first appearance, I remember that I had absolutely no idea what was being said in the address to the haggis. I had to keep a watchful eye on my fellow piper to get the cue for the whisky drinking bit, having been warned beforehand by the older pipers in the band that I MUST drink it in one go.

Later on in my piping career, I brought my pipes over to the UK during a university student exchange scheme. I'd found an agent and he made a booking for me to play at a Burns night in Cambridge, but when I turned up on the allotted night it seemed there had been a mix up about dates and I had been expected the previous night. Not to be deterred, I then went round every pub in Cambridge to see if they might want a piper. I managed to convince one of the pubs and set off that evening to do the job, only to find a few surprises. They had me playing in the cellar bar which had a really low ceiling so I had to play the haggis in whilst crouched down on my knees. Also because the pub had had to buy their haggis at the last minute and all they could get was a very small one, which looked even smaller given the silver platter that it had been placed on.

I have fond memories of all the many Burns night suppers that I have played at; those early ones when I was just learning the ropes as well as subsequently in the years since. We pipers traditionally play 'A Mans a Man for A That' when piping in the haggis. It is an excellent tune for such parading as it has a very structured marching rhythm to it, which generally has the effect of making the audience want to join in with clapping.

In those early days of playing at Burns nights I had no clue as to what the address to the haggis meant or any of the other Robert Burns poems come to that. The gaelic dialect is very strong in Burns' poems and they include specific gaelic words so it was no wonder that I didn't understand them. But, since then, I have taken the time to dig in and read them and understand them properly. I see now how full of humour and pride for the Scottish way of life they are and therefore why Burns night is so loved and

celebrated every 25th January all around the world. I hope that you can find your way to a Burns supper. Listen to 'A Man's a Man for A That'. It will get you in the mood for that heady mixture of good company, warming food, lots of tartan, fine poetry and scottish country dancing. Slainte!

FEBRUARY

2 February: We Will Rock You

Composer: Queen

It is the second of February and you know what that means don't you!? That means that it is national Hedgehog day! What has that got to do with Scotland I hear you ask? Well let me explain. Hedgehogs are a species that are in trouble as their habitats get eroded by us humans. Brian May set up a charity to help these spiky little mammals, it's called 'Project Amazing Grace'. Ok, so why isn't this entry for 2 February all about Amazing Grace then, after all that is a good old Scottish Tune? Amazing Grace. Well let's keep that one for another day. For today, I'll keep going and explain some more. So, Brian May is also the lead guitarist of Queen and Queen wrote We Will Rock You. Get it now?

Ok, it's not obvious how that all links with Scotland, but this is the thing. The bagpipes only have 9 notes to them. No sharps, no flats, just those 9 notes. Yet there have been a whole host of tunes written for just those 9 notes. There is in fact an exceedingly large repertoire of traditional music composed for the bagpipes. But it isn't just traditional music that can be played on the pipes. There are a surprising number of modern pop tunes that also work on the pipes and that is where 'We Will Rock You', by Queen, who has a lead guitarist working to protect Hedgehogs, and on this day of 2 Feb when we are to remember to help hedgehogs, well that is where this all connects together. If you have never heard We Will Rock You played by a pipe band, you are in for something a bit special. Two part harmonies and a rocking base drum make this a thing to remember. Search out some top notch pipers like the Red Hot Chilli Pipers and you will hear what I mean. Even better get along to a highland games and you might even be rewarded by a live performance from an entire pipe band.

Julia Read

14 February: The Clumsy Lover

Composer: Neil Dickie

I was searching for an appropriate date on which to recommend one of Neil Dickie's compositions. I knew that I had to include Neil's work in this anthology of Scottish music mainly because I wanted to make some whimsical and highly amusing comment about the title of his book, namely 'First Book', being so ironically named. It most certainly is not a first book for a newly fledged bagpiper as I'll explain later. But back to the date on which to recommend the works of Neil Dickie. I searched the internet trying to find the date on which 'First Book' was published, hoping to find an actual day and that I thought could make an appropriate day on which to recommend Neil's music to you. But alas I could only find the year of its first publication, 1983; coincidentally I now realise that that was the year that I started to learn the bagpipes back in New Zealand when I was an undergrad in Electronic Engineering. So anyway, having failed to find the actual publication day, I thought I'd look up Neil's Wikipedia page and perhaps find his birthday. But alas he doesn't seem to have a wiki page and about the only biographical information that I could find on this master of modern bagpipe composition is from a site entitled 'celtic fringe' which states that he was born in Glasgow in 1957. So again, alas no date.

But then it struck me, what a dunce I'd been. Many of Neil's compositions are well known and widely played by bagpipers around the world but perhaps the most famous of these is 'The Clumsy Lover' and what better date to recommend such a tune than Valentines night. So, for all you clumsy lovers out there, here it is, Neil Dickie's 'The Clumsy Lover'. Perhaps not a tune to play in the background while you are romancing your beloved with a candle lit dinner as it is a hornpipe full of fast moving and exciting syncopating rhythms. Search out a recording by the 78th Fraser Highlanders and you are in for a real treat. The composition itself, played by a top notch solo bagpiper like Stuart Liddell will give you goose bumps with all the off beats and flying around the chanter that happens. But throw into that an excellent drum core

and a mass of grade 1 pipers such as in the 78th Fraser Highlanders and it is perhaps one of the most exciting tunes in the bagpiping repertoire.

Like all of the tunes in Neil Dickie's 'First Book', 'The Clumsy Lover' is devilishly difficult to play. It has finger movements in it that are so different to many other tunes in the pipers repertoire as well as a complex timing that uses syncopation or off beats in a way that is not often encountered in bagpipe music (at least not before Neil Dickie introduced them to us!). Then to top it all off, it is a hornpipe, so it is played at pretty much break-neck speed. No, it most certainly is not a tune to put in a first tutor book for any musician, but it is one of the most glorious pieces of bagpiping compositions to aspire to being able to play.

Julia Read

21 February: A Meditation on Iona

Composer: Sir James MacMillan

In an interview with Kevin Turley in September 2020, the Ayrshire composer Sir James MacMillan refers to himself as a Catholic composer. It is an intriguing interview in which Sir James explains that many of the composers in the past did so as a way to find God. I have heard this notion before, namely that our Judeo-Christian history was underpinned by a belief that to find God we must explore – explore the world, explore Science, explore the Arts – because God is in everything. These attempts to meet God were the catalyst for many of the great discoveries that came out of this judeo-christian world view. Sir James talks of the opportunity that he feels he has to make this judeo-christian past available to a secular 20th Century world through the music that he composes. It really is a thought provoking interview if you have 30 minutes to spare. It is called 'Music Changes Me'.

However, rather than interviews with the composers, it is the music that this book is trying to introduce you to and for today I am recommending Sir James MacMillan's 1997 composition 'A Meditation on Iona'. It had its world premier on 21 February 1997 at the City Hall Glasgow, performed by the Scottish Chamber Orchestra under the baton of Joseph Swenson. The piece is not about Saint Columba, the Irish abbot that is credited with founding the Abbey on Iona and who spread Christendom to Scotland. Instead it is intended to create a feeling of the island alone. It certainly does that! The place is silence itself interspersed with rugged wildness all bound up with 1000% holyness – something which this piece of music bundles up for you into a 16 minute parcel, that when opened pours out the clanging of abbey bells, great stretches of silence, scratching violins and yet more bells ringing out. It takes some listening to, not because it is hard to digest, but rather because you need to put yourself into a contemplative mood. I had you visit Iona before (24 January). I hope this second visit inspires you to take a trip there yourself. If you do, then I feel sure that you will come to match this piece of music with the impression that Iona leaves on many of its visitors.

26 February: Love is an Arrow

Composer: Aberfeldy

On 26 February 2005 Edinburgh band Aberfeldy had a UK number 60 with their track 'Love is an Arrow', from their debut album 'Young Forever'. Recorded on a single microphone and in mono, it has an urban feel to the sound. In 2015 the track was used in the BBC 3 show Together, a comedy about two young people at the start of their relationship. The track also appears in the 2005 film GamerZ, in fact Alberfeldy contributed 4 of the 7 songs in the movie; including the mellow 'What You Do', the pop tapping alien invasion of 'Heliopalis by Night' and the cheerfully absurd 'Tom Weir'.

The official video that accompanies 'Love is an Arrow' describes the sentiment of the lyrics so well. A love struck eskimo, remembering his old flame, cooking fish over an open fire in his igloo, all alone. He keeps getting postcards from his ex from her travels all around the world, while he is living his lovestruck life all alone. Finally ending with a postcard of the ex with her new boyfriend. Sad, but I guess sometimes life works like that.

The story of the song is poignant, but the rhythm is upbeat, I guess signalling an acceptance of what is and that life goes on. Aberfeldy, a band from Edinburgh and their track 'Love is an Arrow'. Let's hope that they produce many more.

27 February: Bells of Dunblane

Composer: Pipe Major Robert Mathieson

On this day in 1997 The Firearms (Amendment) Act 1997 was given Royal Assent. It seems fitting to me that this tune 'The Bells of Dunblane' is placed here on this day rather than the day of the actual massacre[1]. The Firearms (Ammendment) Act 1997 came into being with the aim of preventing a similar event happening again and it is therefore surely something good that came out of something so dreadfully awful.

Pipe Major Robert Mathieson of the Shotts and Dykehead Pipe Band composed this slow air in memory of the bells of Dunblane cathedral that rang a long tribute to the victims. It is a wonderful composition. You will hear it played the world over by bands in Canada, America, Australia, New Zealand as well as across Europe and of course Scotland.

MARCH

1 March: The Duke of Fife's Welcome to Deeside

Composer: James Scott Skinner

It is March and the dark days of winter are behind us! Well, almost. You know what they say about March. "In like a lion and out like a lamb". That means that we have only got a few weeks left of the roar of winter until we are fully into the dance of the new spring. The dance of the swaying daffodils, the lambs gambling about the Scottish hillsides and the spring sunshine bouncing across the ripples of those oh so cold Lochs. So, to get us in the mood for this dance of Spring, I give to you the Quickstep 'The Duke of Fife's Welcome to Deeside' by James Scott Skinner. If you really want to get into the mood of Spring, Summer even, then check out the version by Scottish musicians Rachel Hair (Clarsach harpist) and Ron Jappy (guitarist) recorded at the Celtic Summer Nights Tour in Austria. There you will find a roaring outdoor fire and people milling around in the warmth of the late evening sun drinking a beer or two. That sunshine and long days will come, have faith.

'The Duke of Fife's Welcome to Deeside' is one of a collection of dances from The Harp and Claymore Collection, published at the start of the 1900s and considered to be James Scott Skinner's magnum opus. The Duke of Fife's Welcome to Deeside is certainly a very popular tune from this collection and if, sorry when, you venture to Scotland, you will hear it played in many a folk club. Hey here's an idea, shall we embrace these last few days of winter and have our spirits travel off to a Scottish folk club now? I am going to suggest Edinburgh. It is a great place to hear live Scottish music and as we are searching out folk music in particular and hoping to hear The Duke of Fife's Welcome to Deeside, then a great place to research where to go seems to be the Edinburgh Folk Club website. I am going to head over to the Leith Folk club and see what that turns up. The club takes over the bar of the Victoria Park Hotel and apparently if there is any Burns on the set list then the audience burst into song. Sounds good to me! So my plan is to briskly walk the 30 minutes from Princess Street, collect a single malt from the bar and hunker down in one of the cosy leather seats to enjoy the warmth of a live folk gig. Feel free to join me. Och, we might even hear Rachel Hair and Ron Jappy play again. What a treat.

5 March: Sam the Skull

Composer: Harry Hagan

We could probably do with more Scottish songs about cats. I am thinking specifically of the Scottish wild cat, those elusive wild felines that live in isolated pockets of the Highlands, with their stripy tails and thick weather proof coat of 30,000 hairs per square cm. In contrast, Sam the Skull, the subject of this humorous Glesga[2] song is not so much of the wild species, more free and easy. Mind you, he is a bit of a rough dude. The song talks of his claws being as strong as crocodile jaws and that prison bars are there to keep Sam out rather than to keep the prisoners in.

Sam the Skull is a much loved song that is sung to children by parents and grandparents in Scotland, so that there is not only an affection but also an awareness for street cats such as Sam. That is the power of song and folklore. Wolves for example are the subject of many stories and songs so that we can kind of relate to them, even if we are a little wary of them. But how many folk songs and stories can you think of that are written about the Eurasian Lynx or the Scottish wildcat? Both are native to Scotland. The Eurasian Lynx has long been wiped out and the Scottish wildcat is an endangered species. There is talk of reintroducing the Eurasian Lynx back into Scotland, but conservationists know that any program like this requires the buy in of people. That is where songs could help. Maybe we need more amusing, toe tapping little songs like 'Sam the Skull', but this time about Scottish wild cats?

Sam the Skull is often associated with Alastair McDonald because of his fun recording of it on his album 'Scottish Laughlines'. But it was actually written by the Scottish musician and composer Harry Hagan and first published in 1981 on the album 'Gaberlunzie: The Travelling Man'. You will be able to find both gentlemen performing 'Sam the Skull' online. While you are searching them down, maybe you could give a thought to Sam's wild cat cousins and look up some of the conservation websites that exist. There may not be any folk songs about Scottish wildcats, but that doesn't mean that we can't help them out, does it?

8 March: The Jeely Piece Song

Composer: Adam McNaughton

If you were going to write a song, what do you think that you might write about? How about a national blood-fat epidemic, or what about MacBeth, or demolishing buildings? No? Well that's too bad because those are the sort of songs that Glaswegian Adam McNaughton writes about and for today I am recommending his song about a multi-storey tower apartment building in inner Glasgow in the 1960s. Yup, if you don't know it already (and if you don't it probably means that you are not Scottish), then I give you 'The Jeely Piece Song'.

The jeely piece of the song's title refers to a jelly (or jam) sandwich and the song sings about what might happen to it if it was thrown out the window. This practise had been alright when the families lived in tenement buildings. The mothers used to wrap jelly sarnies up in paper and throw them out the window to their bairns playing in the streets below. But when the tenements were pulled down and the families moved into the high rise living, lobbing jeely pieces out of a 20 storey window didn't work quite as well. McNaughtan's lyrics have the jeely pieces heading off into space or being caught by low flying planes – no doubt a reference to the high-rise living being so high. It is a comical take on Glasgow life from the 60s. School teacher, McNaughton wrote many other comedic folk songs including the previously referenced 'Cholesterol', 'The Scottish Song' and 'They're Pullin Doon the Building Next Tae Oors'.

There is an online article on Adam McNaughton in the Glasgow newspaper 'The Daily Record', dated 8 March 2018. Worth a read if you would like to find out more about the man.

10 March: All the Bagpipe Tunes Ever

Composer: Multiple composers

Well, you had better like the bagpipes today because today, 10 March, is International Bagpiping day. To celebrate I am cheating slightly and not going to select one individual tune. I mean, how could anyone possibly pick one single tune to represent the bagpipes. Instead, this entry is for all the bagpipe tunes that have ever been written.

I did ask my bagpiping mates to see if there was a common theme from them in terms of which tune best represented international bagpiping day. Alas no common theme emerged. Some pipers went for jigs, others for marches, others for slow airs and then there were those fellows that went for 6/8s. So, just pop onto your favourite streaming service, type in 'bagpipe', and listen to whatever comes up. That will be a perfectly adequate way to appreciate 10 March, International bagpiping day.

26 March: Shang-a-Lang

Composer: Bill Martin – lyrics, Phil Coulter - music

This track comes with a warning. Put it on and you will be wandering around the house all day singing 'and we sang shang-a-lang' in your head. It is a real ear worm.

A hit for the 70s pop group The Bay City Rollers, Shang-a-Lang was written by hit forming musical duo Scotsman Bill Martin and Englishman Phil Coulter. The combination of Martin's lyrics and Coulter's rhythms make this a lasting pop song. I can't speak for every 60 year old's birthday party in Scotland, but I have it on fairly good authority that this one is guaranteed to get on the DJ's playlist.

I hope that you enjoy it. Listen out for the sounds of the Glasgow shipyards. Martin used the clang clang clang of the shipyards to inspire him to the words shang-a-lang. He had grown up there and had completed an apprenticeship as a marine engineer in his youth before then becoming a professional footballer until settling on his childhood passion for song writing.

26 March 2020 sadly marks the day that Bill Martin MBE died at 81. His musical partner Phil Coulter posted a moving tribute to him on social media, referencing the early days of their partnership. So, it feels appropriate to pay a tribute to both of them on this day. In the words of Bill's lyrics 'music like theirs couldn't die'.

APRIL

1 April: Anno/Four Seasons: birds (spring)

Composer: Anna Meredith MBE

It truly is spring now, none of that pretending to be spring that we had back on 1 March. To celebrate this arrival of spring, the piece that I am recommending for you to listen to is by Scottish composer Anna Meredith MBE, namely 'Anno/Four Seasons: birds (spring)'. Another composer that reimagined Vivaldi's Four Seasons was Max Richter who topped the classical charts with his album "Recomposed by Max Richter: Vivaldi – The Four Seasons". The two composers have approached this work rather differently it seems to me. Max Richter's creation pushes and pulls with the timings and seems to turn the melodic lines upside down. Whereas Anna Meredith's creation weaves in an abstractness that is highly characteristic of her other compositions. Much like the American composer Meredith Monk, reviewers have referred to Anna's compositions as uncategorisable; in a category of their own. I really like the 'Anno/Four Seasons: birds (spring)' in the way that it starts off recognisably as Vivaldi then slowly disassembles into what I can only describe as tangential vectors of instrumental sounds. It is like the audio equivalent of watching a flock of birds all neatly stood together on the ground but then as one bird takes to flight, two more follow and for these two that follow, four follow them so that there is this growing mass of birds flying off into the sky, all in different directions.

Julia Read

5 April: The Banjo Breakdown

Composer: Pipe Major Donald MacLeod MBE

Now this is a tune to get your fingers around! Favoured by many of the top solo pipers and A grade bands as part of their competition sets, The Banjo Breakdown jig by PM Donald MacLeod is for intermediate to experienced pipers only. If you are wanting to go to a top notch bagpiping competition, then head on over to the Donald MacLeod Memorial Competition that was set up in 1994 in Stornoway. It is held in early April, around about the 5th, and is in memory of "one of the finest all round pipers of the 20th century"; namely Pipe Major Donald MacLeod MBE.

The Banjo Breakdown appears in PM Donald MacLeod's sixth and last book of tunes and tops off an incredible legacy of tunes that are characteristic of his high standards, musicianship and inventiveness. Tunes such as The Seagull, Dr Ross's 50th Welcome to the Argyllshire Gathering and The Judges' Dilemma have endured and are favoured in the piping repertoire.

7 April: Swerving for Bunnies

Composer: Ailie Robertson

I am not going to lie, I had never heard of this tune before and the only reason that it caught my eye was because of the quirky title. I was browsing through the New Scottish Harp Syllabus for a suitable tune to pluck out for you all to enjoy, and there, in grade 5, within the category of 'recently composed tunes' was this, 'Swerving for Bunnies'. I looked it up on a well known streaming service and there on 7 April was a performance from its Edinburgh born composer and Scottish harpist, Ailie Robertson. Well! What can I say! The piece is a musical delight. I don't know where the bunnies were that Ailie was swerving from, but they were certainly very agile if the variety of rhythms in this piece are anything to go by.

The bunnies start of in a kind of relaxed bluesy sort of way. I can imagine them nibbling by the road side, casually bouncing here and there in their little bunny family groups. Then Ailie's composition has the right hand do all these complicated little runs whilst her left hand pulls out a completely different rhythm in the bass. The bunnies are off! Dashing this way and that. Finally coming to their rest in the last bar with a harpists roll of both hands up the sound board. What a wonderful discovery.

9 April: Oft in the Stilly Night

Composer: words Thomas Moore, music Sir John Stevenson

Oft in the Stilly Night was played on 9 April 2002 outside Westminster Cathedral in London by the Argyll and Sutherland Highlanders as part of the Queen Mother's funeral procession. The mother of Queen Elizabeth II of England born in 1900, laid to rest in 2002. So, as a tribute to the Queen mum, my listing of this hauntingly beautiful Scottish lament is given here on 9 April. 'Oft in the Stilly Night' is a Scottish aire that was penned by Thomas Moore and put to music by Sir John Stevenson. Both Moore and Stevenson were Dubliners, both born in the mid 1700s and both acclaimed for their work; so much so that Sir John Stevenson gained his knighthood because of his music. The tune is referred to by Stephen Dedalus in James Joyce's 'A Portrait of the Artist as a young man'. However, despite its strong Irish associations (Joyce, Moore, Stevenson) it was I believe composed as a Scottish aire, so it feels valid to incorporate it here.

If you search for Oft in the Stilly Night you will come across many versions of it for many instruments and of course it is a song so there are many renditions that involve singers. I particularly like Stuart Burrows' version. Being a Welsh tenor, I feel with the Irish composition of a Scottish aire sung by a Welsh tenor that the combination brings a certain multiculturalism to the lament.

16 April: Scotland the Brave

Composer: Words – Cliff Hanley

Do you really need an introduction to Scotland the Brave? Along with The Flower of Scotland it is sometimes referred to as the Scottish national anthem. Therefore, I am going to operate under the working assumption that you do already know Scotland the Brave and that you have heard the many marvellous versions of it either sung or played on traditional Scottish instruments like the bagpipes, the accordion, the fiddle and the celtic harp. Under that assumption then, I won't refer you off to particular renditions and instead merely mention why I have placed it here on 16 April. 16 April 1746 marks the day when the brave Scottish clansmen of the Jacobite revolution fought on Culloden moor. Unfortunately it was not a win for the Jacobites but it did mark a win for the courage and bravery that followed in trying to keep the Scottish culture alive. It wasn't an easy battle because the English outlawed the wearing of tartan, the speaking of Gaelic and other key elements of Scottish clan life and culture. But the culture did survive. For all those of us that so enjoy the great Scottish culture today, we owe a great debt of thanks to all those people from the 16 April 1746 and onwards for the bravery they showed in keeping this culture alive.

Julia Read

27 April: Moments in Time

Composer: Dame Evelyn Glennie et al

We started this month by remembering the funeral of a beloved Queen. Today we are going to celebrate the start of life by travelling to the town of Pitlochry. Pitlochry is located in Perthshire on the southern tip of the Cairngorm National Park, nestled within deciduous Scottish forests and part of the Scottish Highlands. We will start our tour off in the rather excellent Blair Atholl whisky distillery. Our trip starts with a tour of the facility and ends with some rather fine tasting of their expertly crafted single malt whiskies in the distillery shop. Fresh with the memory of the vision of those giant copper brewing vats and the aroma and taste of the single malts, we leave, with Blair Atholl at our backs, cross the road and make our way to the bridge that spans the fast flowing river Tummel. Pausing on the bridge we look into the rushing waters below as it tumbles over river rocks and boulders. Upstream we see our destination, the Pitlochry dam and visitor centre. It is here that we are going to see the start of new life, as this is where we will find the Salmon ladder. The Salmon ladder at Pitlochry was built in the late 1940s at the same time as the hydro electric dam that was built to stem the Tummel river for the creation of electricity to the region. Building the salmon ladder, meant that all those salmon that used to swim up this river each year to spawn still had a route upwards. Five thousand plus salmon make it through the ladder each year and each salmon can lay anywhere between 5000 to 10000 eggs. The peak of this Salmon spawning is spring, ie April and the exact month that we are in. Lucky us, we're in for a real treat! Off we trot, over the road bridge, past the caravan park on our left and up Foss Road. The road climbs gently through deciduous woods until we get to the first turning on our right and we descend down toward the dam and visitor centre. The fresh spring Highland air fills our nostrils and we hear the tweet tweet of baby birds in the surrounding woods;

we might even spot a red squirrel if we keep our eyes open. All is alive on this fresh spring day. Descending down Port-na-craig Road, we shortly come to the sign for the Iron suspension bridge that sways gently across the river Tummel. Going down to get a closer look, we experience the imposing sight of the Pitlochry dam. The river boulders beneath us on the river bed are a great place for children to slide down and their laughter fills the air. A glance at the river reveals the full swell of salmon fighting their way upstream and which we're going to get a closer look at from the salmon ladder. This is the new life we've come to see. Leaving the Iron suspension bridge from the same direction that we entered it, we turn right, continuing upstream til we reach the pools of the salmon ladder. We witness with our own eyes this mad rush for life and marvel at its sheer wonder. Looking around us and taking in the forests, the air, the sound of the river run, the cool spring sun on our face and the enormity of the engineering feat of the dam, we come to experience this moment in time and the incredible beauty of this place. Now then, what music could possible accompany all of this magnificence? The whisky, the river, the fresh air, the salmon? Well, the title to this day of 10 April may just give it away! [Drum roll] … the music that I have selected for us to listen to as we take in all this wonder is the work of the phenomenal Scottish percussionist Dame Evelyn Glennie. 'Moments in Time' is a soundscape piece and a collaboration between Dame Evelyn Glennie, Barrie Gledden, Chris Bussey and Richard Lacy. It is a taster. An introduction to the work of Dame Evelyn. It is a meditative piece, only lasting 2 ½ minutes, so we may need to replay it a few times as we take our stroll from Blair Atholl to the salmon ladder. It doesn't present the fire of the whisky or the tumultuous rush of the river. Instead, what it is doing for us (I hope) is helping us to get lost in the awe of the beauty of this little spot in bonnie Scotland.

MAY

3 May: Looking at a Rainbow Through a Dirty Window

Composer: Calum Stewart

At this time of year the spring sun is low enough in the sky and the air filled with moisture from morning dew that it must surely be the perfect time to spot a rainbow. Garmouth born composer and musician Calum Stewart wrote the ideal tune to accompany such a Rainbow filled day, 'Looking at a Rainbow Through a Dirty Window'.

I wonder, is a rainbow seen through a dirty window all about the dirty window or the rainbow? Personally I am going to take my morning brew outside, dial up a version of Calum's quartet playing this delightful tune and remind myself that for today all that I will see is the peacefulness of that rainbow.

5 May: Farewell to Stromness

Composer: Sir Peter Maxwell-Davies

To listen to this piece, you really ought to be stood on a North Atlantic ferry deck, leaving the Orkney mainland and making your way out to sea. Facing into the sea breeze, you are all bustled up in a fleece lined raincoat, nursing a mug of steaming hot chocolate in your gloved hands and admiring the Mountains of Hoy looming up out of the cold moody sea. Failing that, just stop what you are doing and contemplate because 'Farewell to Stromness' is a piece that suggests absolute contemplation. It is hauntingly atmospheric and yet redolent of traditional Scottish music with its lilting melody and use of short notes followed by long.

'Farewell to Stromness' is the first interlude of the work, Yellow Cake Revue, by Sir Peter Maxwell-Davies; it had its world premier on 5 May 1990 in Germany. Sir Peter isn't exactly Scottish. Actually he is not Scottish at all (he was born in Lancashire, England), but he did spend a large chunk of his life in Scotland, on Orkney. Much of his work was inspired by his decades living on Orkney, including the Lighthouse opera and this work of The Yellow Cake Revue. He also composed for Scottish musicians such as being Composer Laureate for the Scottish Chamber Orchestra. So, in the same way that I included the non Scottish composer Felix Mendelssohn (14 November) in this book, due to Scotland inspiring his work, I feel that I can justify including Sir Peter too.

I have decided that I won't explain more about what Yellow Cake is or why Sir Peter wrote an entire revue about it. Instead I am going to leave it to you to find out. Maybe when you do, you might ask yourself whether there is a 'yellow cake' type activity going on in your area? If there was, what would you do about it?

12 May: Solitary Citizen

Composer: Malcolm Lindsay

In Malcolm Lindsay's own words much of his music is invisible. He made the remark in April 2015 during a talk that he gave to the Creative mornings HQ in Edinburgh (you can find the session on a well known streaming service, posted on 12 May 2015). The talk was entitled 'Humility vs Ambition: What's the Score'. It is an interesting insight into the work of a TV and film score composer; which is what Malcolm Lindsay is. As he says in his talk he started out life playing in pop groups but then moved into classical music. In fact if you listen carefully you'll hear the lady that introduces him refer to him being a founding member of Deacon Blue (4 June).

When I called up 'Solitary Citizen' on a streaming service, the next tune that got auto played was Vaughan Williams 'Lark Ascending'. They are not the same piece at all of course, but they do have a synergy and seem to create a similar mood. The gentle quiet of Solitary Citizen, stands on its own as a piece of music, but it could equally be the background to a scene from a movie of a peaceful summer's day, much like 'Lark Ascending'.

The track 'Solitary Citizen' is from the album 'Solitary Citizen'. It is recorded by The Royal Scottish National Orchestra and was composed for them by Lindsay. All of the tracks are inspired, but I am recommending this one to you as it happens to be my personal favourite.

29 May: The Atholl Highlanders

Composer: Traditional

Head off to any highland games anywhere in the world and you will hear the tune 'The Atholl Highlanders". That is because it is the music most often played for the highland dancers when they perform the dance that was created in honour of the woman that helped Bonnie Prince Charlie escape, namely 'Flora MacDonald's Fancy'. The Atholl Highlanders is a lovely lilting 4 part bagpipe tune and very appropriate for the swaying and hopping of the Flora MacDonald dance. It can pick up quite a pace though when it is played as a pipe band march. Check out the Black Watch playing it, for example when marching down the Royal Mile in Edinburgh for the opening of the Scottish parliament.

But no mention of the tune 'The Atholl Highlanders' could be complete without referring also to the band who "own" the tune, namely The Band of the Atholl Highlanders. The Atholl Highlanders were granted a right to hold arms by Queen Victoria in 1845 and thus became a private army of the Duke of Atholl, Blair castle, Pitlochry. They are, it seems, the only private army in all of Europe. The annual parade of the Atholl Highlanders started in Queen Victoria's reign and although it has had periods of interruption due to world wars etc, it does still take place every year

at the end of May. 29th May happened to be the date that it takes place in the year 2021; the year in which I am writing this book. Covid permitting is what the website says. Let's hope it can go ahead this year. If you happen to be reading this many years after the 2020/21 Covid apocalypse, why not consider taking yourself along to Pitlochry at the end of May and take part in the festivities. You will be able to experience the Atholl Highlanders parade and gathering; not to mention taste all that whisky and salmon that was mentioned back on the 27th April.

JUNE

1 June: The Gael

Composer: Dougie MacLean

If you are driving around the Highlands and happen to be near Loch Ness on 1 June[3] then why not pop into the Loch Ness visitor centre and have a listen to the original production of 'The Gael'. Composed by Perthshire born Dougie MacLean, The Gael is one of 8 tracks on the album 'The Search' which was written by MacLean specifically for the Loch Ness exhibition. Sandwiched between two tracks that relate to particular Nessie search theories, namely 'The Sixties Vigil' and 'The Underwater Vigil', I am guessing that the track 'The Gael' refers to the theory that the Loch Ness monster might be a giant eel. He (or she) is in there somewhere!

Oh and you may also recognise the Gael from the Last of the Mohicans sound track. But Nessie got there first. This is a very celtic piece of music from a very celtic composer.

2 June: Caledonia

Composer: Dougie MacLean

Now then. Yesterday was all about celtic giant eel music with its synth rhythms, strange rumblings from the deep and celtic fiddle. Today we are going in a completely different direction, although to be honest it wouldn't be that hard to go in a different direction than giant eel music! I am going to have us stick with Dougie MacLean and perhaps one of the best known folk songs. Along with 'The Gael' it is certainly the most well known of songs from Dougie MacLean. Caledonia is nostalgic and warm which makes sense because MacLean wrote it on a beach in his 20s when he was homesick and reminiscing about Scotland (Caledonia being the poetic name for Scotland). It is a song that has stood the test of time and sounds as fresh today as when it was released in the 1970s.

If today you are starting to get out into that warmish sunshine of early June, maybe having some friends round and starting up the bar-b-q for the year, then Caledonia is a great song to add to the playlist. You will be able to search out many renditions of the song, sung by great artists. Personally, I like it when sung by MacLean himself. Think of him playing it for the first time to his Scottish busking mates, they were all near that beach in Brittany together. Apparently, it made them all so homesick that they got on the first ferry home!

Julia Read

3 June: The Braes o' Balquhidder

Composer: Robert Tannahill

Robert Tannahill was born on this day in 1774, 15 years after Robert Burns, and as such he was a contemporary of Burns. Tannahill had a rather sad life it seems to me. It started out quite promisingly but ended up with him taking his own life at the age of 35 when he became despondent. It isn't clear to me why he became so despondent because it seems that his poetry was received with great acclaim. Tannahill started out his life as an apprentice weaver in his dad's shop in Paisley but soon after he finished his apprenticeship he found that he had a talent for poetry. His poetry started to be published in The Scots Magazine and at the turn of the new century he had published a 900 run of his poems and songs in a small book, all 900 of which sold out in a few weeks. Maybe it was a Creative temperament that drove him to drown himself near the Paisley Canal at the age of 35, or maybe it was the pressure of being a 35 year old man and still being at home looking after his elderly mother; his father had died and his 7 siblings had flown the nest leaving Robert as the sole care giver to his mother. Whatever the case, it seems such a loss to the world of this Creative spark.

The Braes o' Balquhidder is a delightful Scottish folk song and one which Paisley born Robert Tannahill left to this world. It is still sung today and is also, I believe, a Scottish Country dance. The lyrics describe an idyllic Highland scene of high summer in what is now known as Loch Lomond & the Trossachs National Park – which is where the mountain slopes of Balquhidder are located; on the banks of Loch Voil. There are many renditions of the tune that you can search out. You may also want to look up 'Wild Mountain Thyme', which was created by Belfast musician Francis McPeake using The Braes o' Balquidder as it's inspiration. Wild Mountain Thyme was first recorded in the 1950s by the McPeake family but it has become so popular that it has since been recorded by numerous artists including The Chieftans, Joan Baez, Mark Knopfler, Ronan Keating, James Taylor and many more. So, I think we have a lot to thank Robert Tannahill for. Not only did he leave this world with a delightful Scottish folk song, his song inspired many other artists to further enrich the world. What a legacy!

4 June: Dignity

Composer: Deacon Blue (Ricky Ross)

If you are late getting your bar-b-q out (2 June) and are just brushing it down today ready for a party this evening, how about this for a cracking '80s tune to add to the playlist. 'Dignity' by Glaswegian band Deacon Blue. Incidentally we've already met a musician associated with Deacon Blue, Malcolm Lindsay (12 May). In his youth, Lindsay played guitar and piano in pop groups and in recent years provided the string arrangements for Deacon Blue's 2012 album Hipster.

Dignity was Deacon Blue's first official release and is one of their most popular songs. It is played at many a Scottish wedding as well as at public events like concerts and even during the Commonwealth Games in 2014 that were held Glasgow. In common with Caledonia, the band's writer of 'Dignity' (Dundee born Ricky Ross) wrote the song whilst not on Scottish shores. He happened to be in Greece at the time and for some reason started thinking about Scottish street cleaners in Glasgow. I know! Azure blue Grecian seas, golden sunsets iridescing the Pentelic marble structures and the smell of moussaka filling the air – why wouldn't someone start thinking of Glaswegian street cleaners. Funny what goes on in our minds sometimes.

The lyrics of 'Dignity' are folkish in a way because they tell a story just like folk songs do. But its music is very definitely in the 80s pop style. It is a song about a street cleaner that is saving his money to buy a dinghy, that he will call 'Dignity', then retire and sail around Scotland. It is in fact why you will see so many boats called 'Dignity' moored in Scottish Lochs.

Go ahead and add this iconic Scottish 80s pop song to that bar-b-q playlist. In fact, while you are at it, why not make a list that has all the songs from the past 3 days. Caledonia, Braes o' Balquhidder and Dignity. A great start to any Scottish party playlist.

7 June: Bruce's Last Breath

Composer: Paul Leonard-Morgan

There isn't much known about where Robert the Bruce was born. Historians know he was born on 11 July 1274 and some put his birthplace at Turnberry Castle in Ayrshire, but others even claim he was born in Essex. The location of his birth may not be clear, but the location of his death is. 7 June 1329 at the Manor of Cardross, near Dumbarton, having secured the Scottish throne, King Robert the Bruce died at the age of 55. His story is one of almost near defeat, many months of hiding out in the islands of Scotland, regrouping and tactical warfare that allowed him to pit brains and strategy to win victory after victory against near impossible odds.

The music that accompanies us today on this remembering of Robert the Bruce is 'Bruce's Last Breath' composed by Scottish composer Paul Leonard-Morgan. A graduate of the Royal Scottish Academy of Music and Drama, he composed the original soundtrack for the BBC series 'A History of Scotland' which goes right back to early millenia looking at the Picts and the Gaels through to modern day Scotland. A great series if you've not watched it. You will find clips on the BBC website. 'Bruce's Last Breath' can be found in the episode 'Bishop Makes King', in the clip 'Robert the Bruce Dies, 1329'.

It is quite a short track 'Bruce's Last Breath', very moody, spirit filled and with the sound of religious chant for a dead King. But don't worry if you feel that it was too short and you are left wanting more. There will be more of Paul Leonard-Morgan's excellent soundtrack to come over the next few days.

Julia Read

8 June: The Legend of Wallace

Composer: Paul Leonard-Morgan

Bruce and Wallace were very close to each other in history. Only 7 years separate Wallace's defeat at Falkirk (1298) and Bruce's start to climb for power in 1305 when it was said that Comyn signed over his rights to the Scottish throne to Bruce. A year later Comyn was dead, murdered in a church by Bruce which then triggered the rushed coronation at Scone palace for Bruce and his Queen. This was followed by the march of the King of England (Edward I and his son) back up to Scotland to 'sort these Scots out once and for all'. The dragon flag was raised by the English, declaring that all chivalric battle practises were ruled out, unfortunately Bruce knew nothing of this and the English slaughtered Bruce's men whilst they were camped up, which was the reason why Bruce decided to resort to guerrilla warfare over the years to come.

Both Bruce and Wallace were fighters for independence. Both were in the same era, but there is something about the Legend of Wallace, a spirit that persists in the air. Maybe because he was the first?

The low flute that introduces this track evokes that spirit of Wallace whirling in the very air. This track brings Wallace in as a whisp of a spirit initially and then we are introduced to the drums, the drums of battle maybe. Like Robert the Bruce after him, Wallace's life was about battling the English for independence. Wallace is all legend, ancient spirit and battle mixed into one and this track echoes that beautifully.

Four and a half minutes of Paul Leonard-Morgan's music, conducting the BBC Scottish Symphony Orchestra. If this music doesn't take your spirit off to Scotland, then I'm not sure what will. 'The Legend of Wallace' can be found in the episode 'Hammers of the Scots', in the clip 'William Wallace'.

9 June: Dunad

Composer: Paul Leonard-Morgan

Bruce came after Wallace. Wallace came well after the picts of the 5th Century, which is what today's track is about. So, I have taken you backwards in time over these past 3 days, and tomorrow I am jumping you forward over a vastness of history to get to Mary Queen of Scots in the 16th Century. My excuse? I don't have one, other than I just like these tracks and feel that they work well in this order. If you want Neil Oliver to guide you on a more chronologically correct path through Scottish history, then take a look at the BBC TV series that accompanies Paul Leonard-Morgan's music.

As this track plays, Neil Oliver has just explained how the Gaels that had come into Scotland from the West and Ireland had built their hill fort at Dunadd. He is climbing up through what used to be the entrance to the fort and the videographer's drone shot pulls out to reveal the hill fort of Dunad, rising up out of the vast flatness of Moine Mhor, which means the big bog. If you can't find the clips from this series, that is what is happening as this music plays and if you listen to the music you can almost hear that vision of the camera pulling out to show the landscape.

The driving drum beats at the start of this track seems to suggest the urgency of the Gaels to build their hill fort to fend off the Picts. With the brass section coming in half way through creating the expansiveness of the terrain that Dunad was positioned in. The track ends quietly, maybe symbolic of the Gaels leading a semi harmonious life with the Picts. Afterall, as Neil Oliver says the Picts and Gaels weren't always battling each other and were often allies.

'Dunad' can be found in the episode 'The Last of the Free', in the clip 'Gaelic Culture in Early Scotland'.

Julia Read

10 June: Mary Queen of Scots

Composer: Paul Leonard-Morgan

This is the last of Paul Leonard-Morgan's tracks from 'A History of Scotland' that I shall be recommending. Perhaps it was unfair of me to focus so much on his work on this particular TV show. He has after all composed so much for film and TV. For example the soundtracks for Walking With Dinosaurs, Dynasty (the remake), The Grand Tour, as well as for computer games. But I suppose that I just wanted to introduce you to his work and as this is a book on Scotland, it seemed appropriate to focus on his music for 'A History of Scotland'.

This last track was written for Mary Queen of Scots. Am I allowed to say she had a turbulent life? Married at 15, then 2 husbands die on her culminating in a 3rd marriage to a rather dubious chap and then be imprisoned for 18 years by her half sister Elizabeth before being beheaded, certainly seems pretty turbulent to me! This track though is quite light. It has the lightness of youth and the swell of a sea. Perhaps it is a reflection of Mary's early years when she was young and innocent? Maybe that is a nice way to think of Mary, sent off to France over the sea to grow up in peace and tranquility full of hope for her yet to be determined future as Queen.

'Mary Queen of Scots' can be found in the episode 'Project Britain', in the clip 'Mary, Queen of Scots and the European Reformation'.

11 June: Ally's Tartan Army

Composer: Andy Cameron

The mid 70s was quite the time for tartan scarves on the BBC Hit parade show, Top of the Pops. Teeny boppers in platform shoes and flared trousers, dancing in the audience, holding up tartan scarves with both arms held above their heads, swaying their tartan from side to side as the band on stage gave it their (Scottish) all. There was Rod Stewart, The Bay City Rollers and in this case Andy Cameron with 'Ally's Tartan Army'. Tartan was so on trend in fact that even the Wombles got in on the act when they appeared on Top of The Pops! Their leader, Great Uncle Bulgaria, sported a tartan cape, tartan hat and tartan slippers. Then there was Cairngorm MacWomble The Terrible who wore a tartan plaid wrapped around his body and a sporran with a 'W' emblazoned on it. There is a rumour that there was a Nessie womble who was an acqua sub-species of the larger land womble genre. Apparently, she is actually the basis for the Loch Ness legend and looks with scorn at other rumours such as giant eels (see 1 June). But this really is only a rumour and you will have to reach your own conclusions.

Anyhoo, I digress! Back to Andy Cameron and Ally's Tartan Army. Andy Cameron was a Scottish comedian and in 1978 he wrote a fun little song in support of Scotland who had secured a place in the FIFA Football World Cup. He appeared on Top of the Pops on 9 March 1978 in readiness for the World Cup that was to start in June that same year. It is a song full of promise. Of how Scotland were going to win and bring the Cup home to glory. Unfortunately, Scotland got knocked out in the first round and 11 June 1978 was their last game, which they happened to win against Holland, but their previous two games on 3rd and 7th June hadn't been enough to get them through.

The song is sung as a football chant today, so it is still very well known. But head on back to the original of Andy Cameron on Top

Julia Read

of the Pops 9 March 1978. It is a sight to behold.

12 June: Donald Where's Your Troosers

Composer: Neil Grant (Iain MacFayden) – music, Andy Stewart - words

If you are still in for a bit of fun Scottish music after Ally's Tartan Army from yesterday, then how about this offering of 'Donald Where's Your Troosers'. It was sung by Andy Stewart and reached No. 1 in Canada in the 60s when it was first released! It is definitely a bit of fun and Stewart's recording of it is a hoot with his impersonations of a young naïve guy from Skye, finishing up singing in a broad Scottish accent, after having travelled through a version of it sung in the style of Elvis. The song was re-released in 1989 and became a No. 4 hit in the UK.

Stewart wrote the words and Iain MacFayden (whose musical composer nom-de-plume was Neil Grant) wrote the music. They were both associated with the 60s BBC TV variety show 'The White Heather Club'. Stewart was its presenter and MacFayden, who was Head of Light Entertainment for BBC Scotland, was the founder of the show. If, like me, you are a child of the 60s then this sort of music will bring back fond memories of sitting round the TV on a Saturday night watching shows like this with your folks before you were packaged off to bed. Ah, fond memories.

Julia Read

13 June: Crags of Tumbledown Mountain

Composer: Pipe Major Jim Riddell

In June 1982 I was in the middle of my first year at Engineering School in Auckland New Zealand. Earlier that year I had convinced my sister that we just had to join a pipe band and learn to play the bagpipes. So we did. We joined a band formed up of retired Army pipers that had emigrated to Auckland and we absorbed it all. The Falklands war was a constant item on the news, but seemed so distant to me as far as our lives in Auckland were concerned. It hadn't moved us. But in December the following year (1983), my sister and I returned to England for a 3 month stay. We took our pipes with us and looked around for a pipe band to join. This is where the Falklands war came into our lives because the band were playing this new tune that we had never heard before. It was so catchy. It was melodic and innovative and everyone could play it. It sounded stirring when a solo piper played it, but that was nothing compared to when the full drum core joined in. It is a tune that when you hear it it just makes your heart swell and your feet want to march. 'What is that great tune?' I must have asked and our new pipe major handed me the music sheet 'The Crags of Tumbledown Mountain' by Pipe Major Jim Riddell. 'The Crags of Tumbledown Mountain', 'Banjo Breakdown' (5 April) and 'Clumsy Lover' (14 February) are synonymous to me with that period. It is when I discovered these wonderful tunes. It seemed to me that every piper could play them and I wanted to too.

So what is this tune 'The Crags of Tumbledown Mountain' and who was Pipe Major Jim Riddell? Well, PM Jim Riddell was in the Scots Guard 2nd Battalion and in 1982 he was fighting in the 10 week battle of the Falkland Islands. It was a territorial conflict between Argentina and the UK and ended on 14 June 1982. On 13 June the Scots guards were involved in a hand-to-hand combat attack on the Argentine position on Tumbledown Mountain. As the battle ended, Pipe Major Jim Riddell reportedly took out his pipes on the summit and played his composition 'The Crags of Tumbledown Mountain'. I think that he must have written it earlier during the conflict because by all accounts it was a tune that was heard so often during the war that it became almost a national anthem of the Falklands.

Please do look this one up as it is an absolute gem in the piping world. Try searching out for a massed bands version of it, for example at the Berlin Tattoo. I feel sure that you will have the same reaction to it as I did when I first heard it. It is a tune that grows the spirit.

Julia Read

19 June: The False Bride

Composer: Unknown

The False Bride is a delightful folk song that I suggest you just listen to and not try to bend your mind around the many aspects of confusion that surround it. If you got hooked on the Outlander series back in January (4 Jan) and have been binge watching it ever since then you may well have made it to Series 4 which is when Richard Rankin as Roger sings this song to Sophie Skelton as Brianna; make a mental note that Brianna is the daughter of James FRASER and Claire FRASER.

Oh dear, I have teased you now with a bit of the solution to the puzzle of this song – that whole Fraser thing. Now then, if you really don't want to suffer the fate of many others over the past 300 years that have been trying to puzzle the meaning of this song that has long been known as the oldest riddle in Britain, then can I suggest that you stop reading now.

But if you are a sucker for punishment, then here you go, but don't say I didn't warn you!

So the producers of Outlander are really into their details it seems because they seem to be concurring with a theory by Canadian author Jack Whyte that the lyrics refer to the ancient 'strawberry' clans that geographically link to Dogger Bank. Dogger Bank is a submerged land bank between Scotland, Netherlands and Brittany that used to have rich fertile forests but got flooded 10,000 years ago. The land territories that link with Dogger bank were inhabited by the Scottish FRASER clan, the Dutch Frisian people and the Brittany celtic clan who call themselves 'les gens de la fraise" (the people of the strawberry). All three clans – Scottish, Dutch, French – have the strawberry as their clan symbol. That explains the strawberry part of the song (and the forests of ye olde Dogger bank pre-flooding), but it doesn't really explain the question and answer that relates to strawberries that is plonked in the middle of the song.

The song tells the story of unrequited love. Having watched his love get married to another, he takes his own life. At the wedding though, the singer is sad to have lost his love and is asked 'how many strawberries grow in the salt sea?' to which he replies 'how many ships sail through the forest?'. What do you think this means? Yes, sure the strawberries refer to ancient clans and the salt sea possibly refers to the land mass that got flooded, but still, why these two questions?

That isn't where it stops with the puzzles in this song. There is no real clarity around who wrote it, when it was written or what country it belongs to – is it a Scottish or English folk song. I can't find conclusive evidence, but you know, it sort of suits the purposes of this book to claim it as Scottish, plus it is so lovely that I just really wanted you to hear it, so I'm just going to leave it right here for you to enjoy.

Julia Read

21 June: Heartwood

Composer: Karine Polwart, Seckou Keita

I only discovered 'The Lost Words: Spell Songs' a few days ago after speaking with a bagpiping customer of mine. I had put him onto the Robyn Stapleton version of Ae Fond Kiss and we had a bit of an exchange about Scottish music when he suggested that I listen to The Lost Words: Spell Songs. The whole work is a musical composition based on the acclaimed book 'The Lost Words: A Spell Book' by Robert MacFarlane and Jackie Morris. It is a book of spells on words about nature like seedscatter, acorn, heron, heartwood. MacFarlane and Morris had noticed that these were being removed from the Oxford junior dictionary and replaced with words like broadband and pixel. The book began as a protest against the removal of everyday nature words but grew into a broader protest about the loss of the natural world. It has won numerous prizes and was shortlisted in 2017 for Britain's favourite books of all time on the natural world.

The Spell Songs work, takes the book of The Lost Words: Spells and based on this created 14 tracks. It is a collaboration between acclaimed musicians, some of which you will recognise from the Scottish music scene, namely Julie Fowlis, Karine Polwart, Kris Drever, Rachel Newton. The rest of the song writing troupe from Spell Songs are English, Kerry Andrew, Beth Porter, Jim Molyneux and Senegal born Seckou Keita.

I am going to start you off with Heartwood. It is just one of the many wonderful tracks from Spell Songs. Karine Polwart and Seckou Keita combine on Heartwood to create a melody that has traditional Scottish folk motifs as well as the distinctive sound of the Kora from Seckou Keita. It is short but an absolute delight and will, I hope, be a springboard for you to discover the other tracks from Spell Songs.

24 June: Highland Wedding

Composer: Donald Cameron[4]

Highland Wedding is a 2/4 march played by highly experienced competition pipers and graded as very difficult. I say this to provide some context to the story that I relate to you on 8 August of my experiences with it from when I was a young piper. It is not a tune to be tackled lightly. Having said that, it is an absolutely delightful tune to listen to. It doesn't sound difficult at all to the listener, it sounds light and lilting and highly appropriate to the mood of a Scottish Wedding. Which is probably why it was chosen to be played at Mrs Hughes wedding to Carson on Downton Abbey. You can hear it as they both recess down the aisle after the ceremony and the piper stands outside parading them out of the church. You can hear a full version of all the 6 parts on an album entitled 'The World's Greatest Pipers, Vol. 13'. I have a great fondness for the tune. I like the way the melodic lines climb upwards in a seesawing motion almost like the swish and sway of the bride's dress as she and her groom walk joyfully down the aisle.

We are listening to it here on Midsummers day. What better day could there be for a tartan highland wedding.

JULY

1 July: A Man's a Man for A That

Composer: Words – Robert Burns, Tune - traditional

We are visiting 'A Man's a Man for A That' for a second time (see 25 Jan for the first time). The reason that this repeat feels justified is for two reasons. Firstly this tune is almost the national anthem of Scotland so it is worth repeating. Secondly I wanted to note a point in Scottish history on 1 July where this tune became a seminal moment, namely the opening of the Scottish parliament on 1 July 1999.

Maybe on 25 Jan you looked up a rendition of 'A Man's a Man for A That' that was played on the bagpipes and that was wholly appropriate as it was Burns night and this is the tune that pipers play when piping in the Haggis. For today though, I am going to suggest that you look up the sung version of this song. Specifically the rendition that Sheena Wellington, the acclaimed traditional Scottish singer, sang on 1 July 1999. The reason? Well, the 1 July 1999 was the first opening of the Scottish parliament since 1707. The Act of Union 1707 united Scotland and England, forming the UK and its government. This brought great change to Scottish cities and in time great prosperity. In Edinburgh for example 1785 saw the opening of South Bridge which was the city's first purpose built shopping parade and at that time was one of the fanciest shopping parades in all of Europe. Some 300 years later, in 1997, the Scottish people voted in a devolution referendum in favour of the creation of a Scottish Parliament with devolved powers from the parliament of England. 1999 saw the establishment of the first Scottish parliament for 292 years and Queen Elizabeth II presided over the opening of the Parliament building, which is located near Holyrood house in Edinburgh.

Sheena Wellington sang 'A Man's a Man for A That' to the gathered house and encouraged all to join in on the last verse. In a 2019 interview posted on twitter, Sheena says that she had never been so emotional singing a song in her life. It really was quite a moment. Well worth witnessing if you have not already seen it.

Julia Read

3 July: She Moved Through the Fair

Composer: Irish traditional

In five days time, on 8 July, you are going to land on Baker Street by Gerry Rafferty, perhaps the most famous single for this Paisley born and raised singer song writer. But on our way to this huge hit for Rafferty, I thought that we might take a potted history through his musical influences and early homelife. The reason? Well he grew up in Scotland in the 1950s and 60s, surrounded by the Scots/Irish music in the same way that many other Scottish musicians have and he also experienced the working class life in his youth yet crossed class/income barriers as an adult, much like Lulu (3 November) and Billy Connolly (8 January). So, it makes for an interesting look at not only the musical influences for Rafferty but many other contemporary Scottish musicians as well.

Today we are starting with Rafferty's early childhood and the song that his mother used to sing so well[5], 'She Moved Through the Fair'. Rafferty's mother (Mary Skeffington) was Scottish and his father Irish. Take a listen to this beautiful Irish aire that Mary Skeffington sang to young Gerry. Listening to Caitlin's version of 'She Moved Through the Fair', for me, there is something about the strong melodic lines that evoke a similar atmosphere to Baker Street.

4 July: The Last Rose of Summer

Composer: Thomas Moore

Yesterday described a tune that Rafferty's mother sang. Today we are moving on to tunes that Rafferty and his brothers used to sing. Rafferty says that from a very young age he and his two older brothers used to sing 3 part harmonies on traditional Scottish/Irish songs, always performing at parties for Christmas, New Year and Birthdays.

Thomas Moore was exceptionally gifted according to Rafferty. Moore was an Irish poet and lyricist of some political and religious influence in his time (1779 – 1852), but I'll not go into that! For his song writing, he is most remembered for 'The Minstrel Boy' and 'The Last Rose of Summer'. Both are lovely, but it is July, we are in Summer, so it seems appropriate to talk of roses rather than a minstrel boy. Maybe it isn't yet the last rose of summer on 4 July, in fact by the 4 July they are just about reaching their peak in the Northern Hemisphere, but let's have a listen anyway.

You could search out a performance of 'The Last Rose of Summer' by a young tenor such as Emmet Cahill and imagine Rafferty or one of his brothers singing this as a solo, just after they have sung 'The Mountains of Mourne' in close harmony.

5 July: My Apartment

Composer: The Humblebums

You have been embarking on a 6 day tour of Gerry Rafferty's musical influences and I have not mentioned any music composed by him yet. I am still not going to do it today because although he did compose a lot of the music that the Humblebums performed, I thought that I would refer you off to a composition by the other singer song writer in the Humblebums, namely Billy Conolly (8 January). Rafferty and Conolly set up the band from Glasgow with guitarist Tam Harvey in 1965, but Harvey didn't stay long and soon it was just Rafferty/Conolly in this Scottish rock folk band. They had quite some success with tunes like Shoeshine Boy and Saturday Round About Sunday. Today you are listening to 'My Apartment' which features Conolly as lead singer.

'My Apartment' is a jolly mix of guitar, drums, banjo and piano. Despite the jolly music, I am going to go out on a limb here and risk drawing a parallel between the lyrics of the song and the alienation that often accompanies creatives like Conolly and Rafferty. The lyrics tell of a man that goes out into the world, experiences a bit of it but then as soon as he encounters anything just a bit off he wants to run back to his apartment. It seems to be a message of hiding, of blanking the world out. Which is kind of sad, but quite a frequent human condition it seems.

That world out there can be a fearful place and certainly makes me want to run 'back to my apartment' sometimes. But for today, I am bounding out the door with the jolly spirit of the jangling guitars, piano and drums from this track. I am going to go meet with people and embrace the wonder of lil' ole planet Earth. How about you?

6 July: Mary Skeffington

Composer: Gerry Rafferty

Rafferty left the Humblebums at the height of their success to set out on his own solo career. His first album 'Can I Have My Money Back' included this track in dedication to his mother 'Mary Skeffington'.

She was a Scottish lass, Mary and in a fairly often encountered marital combo, this Scottish lass married a young Irish chap. Both were songsters in that they sang their Scots/Irish songs around the house when Rafferty and his two brothers were young. Unfortunately Rafferty recounts that it wasn't a happy lot as his Irish dad was an alcoholic and his mum used to take him and his brothers out of the house and wait in the streets when his dad came home so they could avoid a beating.

'Mary Skeffington' is a song from a grown man, seen through the eyes of a young boy, to the young wife that was then his mother, offering her hope and guidance for how to survive this tough season of her life. To have included this song on his first solo album, I think it is clear that creating a dedication to his mother was important to Rafferty. It may not be his most well known song, but the obvious importance of it to him is why I have included it here.

Julia Read

7 July: Stuck in the Middle with You

Composer: Steelers Wheel

Gerry Rafferty started out as a child listening and singing Scots/Irish music, then as a teenager he formed a band (The Humblebums, 1965 – 71) then went solo ('Mary Skeffington'), then formed another band – Steelers Wheel. Steelers Wheel were a Scottish rock/folk group formed in Paisley 1972 by two old school friends Gerry Rafferty and Joe Egan.

Rafferty wrote the lyrics for 'Stuck in the Middle With You' and the tune was formed with fellow band member Joe Egan. The song is about a music industry cocktail party told as a parady in a Bob Dylan style. Mind you one might say that the phrase 'stuck in the middle' was a prediction of what was to come for Rafferty because when he left the band, then went back, then left again finally in 1975 he ended up in a 3 year legal battle with them that prevented him releasing any more work. Maybe that is why he stayed out of bands for the rest of his musical career. More on that legal battle tomorrow.

If you happen to be in a situation in your life where you are surrounded by clowns, put this track on with a little smile of acceptance and do a Hal from Malcom in the Middle – hand jiving on the sofa to 'Stuck in the Middle With You' while all around utter chaos breaks out.

8 July: Baker Street

Composer: Gerry Rafferty

We have arrived! Baker Street written by Gerry Rafferty (all of it! even the saxophone riff) and placed here on 8 July because that is the date in 1978 that the album that it was on, 'City to City'[6] toppled Saturday Night Fever from the US charts.

'City to City was Rafferty's second solo album. He released it after what must have seemed like a never ending 3 year legal battle trying to free himself from the contract he had whilst in Steelers Wheel. He is quoted as saying that he used to wander around the streets of London feeling alone and in despair as to whether he'd ever get through it – Baker Street is named after London's Baker Street and has lyrics in it that relate to feeling lonely in a big city.

There is much written about Baker Street. How Rafferty said in an interview that it earned him £80k a year. How the claim by the saxophonist Raphael Ravenscroft that he wrote the famous sax riff was finally disputed by evidence of Rafferty playing the riff in the demo tape on guitar. And of the irony of the track in that it is rebellious about fame yet it led to Rafferty becoming a huge star. You can certainly find all of that back story very easily. Whilst you are searching out Baker Street, why not take a listen to the first track, The Arc, on the album and you will find yourself going back full circle to the Scots/Irish folk music of Rafferty's youth.

Julia Read

10 July: Psalm 16: 8 – 9

Composer: Gaelic psalm singers

On the day of John Calvin's birth, we are going to listen to a legacy that his theological principles left on the music of Scotland, namely Gaelic psalm singing. Gaelic psalm singing is mostly still sung in the outer Hebrides and is, I believe, where the lined-out singing of Baptist North Carolina stems from. In accordance with Calvinism, the sound is voice only and unaccompanied by any instruments. The congregation is led by a Precentor who starts off the chant, followed by the whole congregation who hear the tune but sing it according to their own interpretation. The precentor and congregation alternate in their singing so the whole composition has this ebbing and flowing to it – think the Northern lights put to voice. The effect is beautiful and eerie.

15 July: In a Big Country

Composer: Big Country (Stuart Adamson)

In my earlier years I didn't really listen to popular music. What I heard mostly was the melody, mostly the chorus or any catchy little riffs, certainly not the lyrics. So, when I dialled up 'In a Big Country' in order to write about it in this book, I recognised it as a familiar song. It had been a hit in the 1980s when the album that it was on had its release – 'The Crossing', 15 July 1983. The guitar riffs in the bridge must have resonated with me as a teenager. Not only because they are really catchy but also because I had been learning the bagpipes and it seems that Big Country used to purposely use their guitars to create bagpipe sounds. They were of the MTV generation and it made this particular track a huge hit in the USA. MTV was so huge that it was hard to avoid and so this track is definitely a song that I associate with that 1980s music era.

As I've grown older, I find myself digging into the lyrics more. I never really took the time to bother with the meaning, but I do now. What do the lyrics of 'In a Big Country' say to you? I had sat down to research this entry after having just had my breakfast. I had watched a video from a well known streaming service that was entitled 'Quit Your Day Job and Live Out Your Dreams by Dr. Ken Atchity'. I don't know about you, but I find when I have an enquiring mind and keep working to be creative then random things miraculously become connected. The lyrics of 'In a Big Country' mean exactly that to me – live out your dreams. Stay alive. I don't have to be the biggest and the best ('getting flowers to grow in a desert'), just live my dreams and find the positives in the world around me even if the situation is bad ('seeing sunshine in winter[7]').

Big Country were formed in 1981 in Dunfermline, Fife – just over the Forth bridge a few miles north of Edinburgh. They are still

Julia Read

touring today, albeit in a different line up to the original. There are known reasons for that and the band's history tells that story. For me though, personally, I want to take the message from this song – stay alive, find sunshine in the winter and it doesn't matter if my dreams aren't so revolutionary that they could grow roses in a desert, just find a way to live them.

17 July: I'm Gonna Be (500 miles)

Composer: Craig Reid, Charlie Reid

It is exactly 6 months ago today that I last spoke of Craig and Charlie Reid from the Proclaimers (see 17 January). That time I suggested that their song 'I'm On My Way' might be a good chant for any New Year's resolutions that you might have set. So how is it going with the resolutions? Are you still on track? Och well, no matter. Have a listen to 'I'm Gonna Be' anyway, see if it reinvigorates those aspirations from January.

'I'm Gonna Be' is the most famous of the Proclaimers songs. Apparently, it earns 5 times more in royalties than anything else in the Proclaimers catalogue. It was a hit when it first appeared in 1988 and then it achieved even more success when it was included in 1993 in the soundtrack of the US film 'Benny and Joon'. It has appeared in US shows like The Simpsons and Family Guy. Frankly, why wouldn't it, it is a brilliant tune.

If your New Year's resolution was to get healthier then how about resuscitating it as we go into the last half of the year? Put this track on, tie up those shoe laces on your walking shoes and get out there for those 500 miles. da da da da …..

23 July: Major Thomas of Cairnleith

Composer: Lindsay Ross

If you needed proof that Scottish culture is appreciated the world over then try typing 'The Wishing Well Beltane Fires' into an online search engine. What you will find will be a video taken at the Russian Festival of Scottish Country Dancing (!!!) in Novgorod, May 2015, showing the dance school 'Beltane Fires' demonstrating the delightful Scottish country dance The Wishing Well. If for one minute you suspend the fact that the walls are plastered in Saltire flags, that the women are dressed in tartan and the men in kilts and instead put your mind into what you might imagine an eastern European country might be, then with this in mind concentrate on listening to the music – does it sort of sound Russian/Eastern European to you? It would be no surprise if it did because the tune's composer, Lindsay Ross, was influenced in his youth by Polish soldiers that were billeted in his town of Kirriemuir. They encouraged the young accordion player so that he became proficient and confident enough to form his own band at just the age of 12.

Ross was born in Kirriemuir, a delightful gateway to the Highlands just north of Dundee. Incidentally, Kirriemuir was also the birthplace of Scottish novelist JM Barrie, which is why you will find a Peter Pan theme park there when you visit. Back to Lindsay Ross though. Born in the 1930s, he trained as a carpenter, but music was his passion and what with the rise of TV and radio after WWII, music became his profession and he was very much a part of the 1950s light entertainment scene, appearing on the BBC's TV 'The Kilt is My Delight' in 1960 and the Jimmy Logan show in 1957.

Ross left his mark on this world. Not only through the huge collection of Scottish dance music that his band recorded/composed, but also because of his later work in restoring grade B listed cottages. He was awarded a Civic Award by the Historic Buildings Scotland for the four cottages that he restored in the historic village of St Vigeans.

Here is an idea for you. If you are planning a little tour of Scotland, why not consider a Lindsay Ross themed driving trip? Start in his birth place, 'the wee red toon' Kirriemuir (take the kids to the Peter Pan theme park while you are there), then do the 20 mile drive to the historic coastal town of St Vigeans. Visit Arbroath Abbey and the dramatic Abroath cliffs. Then bundle yourselves up in the car again and set off for a drive up the 50 mile coast road to Aberdeen and visit His Majesty's Theatre where Ross and his band played on the Jimmy Logan show in the 1950s. Buy yourself an album of Ross's Scottish Dance Music and you will have the perfect accompaniment to a fabulous wee journey.

Julia Read

24 July: Wishing Well

Composer: Angus MacPhail

Major Thomas of Cairnleith (23 July) is the recommended Strathspey tune for the Scottish Country Dance 'The Wishing Well'. In fact you will find it very hard to find a recording of just the tune of Major Thomas of Cairnleith and the easiest way to find it is to look up any video demonstrating the dance 'The Wishing Well'. This tune is so closely associated with the dance in fact that people often refer to it as 'The Wishing Well', however you now know differently and so will be able to confidently declare "oh yes that is a common mistake, people often think that the tune for the Wishing Well is called The Wishing Well, but it is actually a tune composed by Lindsay Ross called Major Thomas of Cairnleith".

Having cleared that up and given you that little nugget of Scottish knowledge, today we are going to look at another Scottish connection with wishing wells and this time it is a tune that has the actual title 'Wishing Well'. If you enter 'Wishing Well' into a search engine you'll probably find Terence Trent D'Arby's song, but go right on past that (oh ok, have a listen, it is iconic after all) and head on over to the song by Scottish rock band Skipinnish.

Angus MacPhail of Skipinnish wrote 'Wishing Well' as a tribute to Eilidh MacLeod from Barra who was sadly killed in the Manchester Arena Bombing in 2017. Eilidh was 14 years old at the time and one of the 22 youngsters that were killed in the terrorist attack at that Ariande Grande concert in 2017. The community of Barra erected a statue in her honour and the profits from Skipinnish's song 'Wishing Well' helped to fund its construction. Eilidh was a piper in the Sgoil Lionacleit Pipe Band and so the statue is of a young bagpiper girl, with pipes at rest, holding her hand out to a young boy who is wanting to learn. Eilidh was also a talented highland dancer and so I feel sure that she would have also danced Scottish Country Dances, maybe even The Wishing Well. So we've come full circle – the dance – the tribute – the Wishing Well.

It is impossible to imagine the grief of losing a daughter so young and with such promise. Words escape me. Wishing Well; Rest in Peace Eilidh.

25 July: Margaret's Waltz

Composer: Pat Shuldham-Shaw

If you are heading off to a summer Scottish wedding today and your bride and groom have organised a Scottish Ceilidh band for the night's entertainment, then you may well hear this lovely lilting Waltz. I will get this said right up front though, Pat Shuldham-Shaw wasn't Scottish. He was from Shakespeare country actually, Stratford Upon Avon, but he gave so much to the celtic (Irish and Scottish) music canon that he definitely deserves a mention as far as I am concerned. Also, a lot of the ceilidh bands will play this waltz, plus the tune itself has the musical style of the Shetlands about it (something which Pat Shaw was renowned for), so it definitely has a strong Scottish association and deserves to have you listen to it on this bright sunny July day as you head off to that wedding.

I am going to recommend that you look up the video of it performed by Mark Knopfler and his band. Then I am just going to leave it there. Enjoy. Hope you have a lovely time at that wedding. Huge congratulations to the bride and groom. I will see you tomorrow for a late breakfast and another great piece of Scottish music.

26 July: Coilsfield House

Composer: Nathaniel Gow

Did you go to that Scottish wedding yesterday? Well here is another tune that you may have heard 'Coilsfield House'. Not a dance number, rather a slow aire, possibly played in a quiet time by the band, maybe when the evening buffet was laid on. And if you didn't get to a wedding yesterday, either way 'Coilsfield House' is a lovely gentle tune to accompany a lazy hazy summer's morning, with a late leisurely breakfast consisting maybe of an Aberdeen Rowie[8] and a few teaspoons of jam made with Scottish Raspberries.

Nathaniel Gow wrote Coilsfeld house. They were a prodigious lot, the Gow family. It is probably more accurate to refer to them as the Gow musical dynasty. They were certainly the most celebrated fiddlers of their time (the 1700s). Nathaniel's father, Niel Gow is renowned to have been THE most famous fiddler of the 18th Century. Both Nathaniel and Niel were prolific composers, and Nathaniel's son Neil also composed a number of tunes. The Gow's legacy can be heard in most of the Scottish country (and ceilidh) dance tunes that are played today, along with some of the other great fiddler composers of the 18th Century namely William Marshall, Donald Dow and Robert MacIntosh.

But today you are not Ceilidh dancing. Today you are being peaceful and Coilsfield House is entirely appropriate to such a mood. Coilsfield House is often a tune learnt by beginner fiddlers and it is definitely a core tune in the fiddler's repertoire. If you would like to hear a true professional play it, then check out the Canadian fiddler Natalie MacMaster. Take a bite out of that Rowie, sip your coffee, laze back, enjoy the sunshine and just let Natalie's playing soak right into your day.

31 July: We Are stars

Composer: Callum Beattie

If you are looking to discover a great singer and rising star, think Coldplay's Chris Martin with a slight Scottish accent, then look no further than Callum Beattie. His appropriately titled first single "We are Stars" is a fabulous indie song, ideal for listening to when on a drive. I say it is appropriately titled because Edinburgh born singer songwriter Callum must surely be a rising star. With great songs like this then that surely is inevitable.

AUGUST

8 August: Cumha Mhic an Toisich (or Mackintosh's Lament)

Composer: Piobaireachd - Ancient

It is fairly shocking that an entry on Piobaireachd (or Pibroch) has not made it into this volume until August. It is after all the classical music, the ancient music, of the Great Highland Bagpipes. The reason for waiting until August until referencing a Piobaireachd is to be able to mark with respect a Duke from Deeside that we met before on 1 March, the Duke of Fife. It was on this day, 8 August, 1912 that the 1st Duke of Fife, Alexander Duff was laid to rest after a tragic incident when the family's ship went aground near Morocco. Alexander Duff was given the title of 1st Duke of Fife when he married Queen Victoria's granddaughter Princess Louise and it seems from various accounts that he was highly regarded as a notable personality of Upper Deeside, where he and his family lived for many years. The Glasgow Herald (online) gives an account of the funeral procession in Braemar, noting the hundreds of people that lined the river Dee and how the Piobaireachd 'Mackintosh's Lament' was brought into the proceedings...

"The casket was here removed from the hearse to a bier, and in a few minutes the wail of the bagpipes, the Mackintosh's Lament, which was the favourite pibroch of the late Duke, was the melancholy announcement to the hundreds of people who lined the southern bank of the Dee that the final portion of the sad journey had begun."[9]

I have also been somewhat reluctant to write about Piobaireachd

Julia Read

because of a slight fear that I describe it incorrectly. It is highly regarded and a fine fine art amongst a few of the very best pipers, so I do not want to do it a disservice. I remember when I first heard it and remember how totally moved I was by it. I was a 19 year old bagpiper that had been playing pipes only for 3 months when I rather foolishly convinced my pipe major that I'd like to enter a competition playing all 6 parts of Highland Wedding. But that is another story and the key thing here is that this was the highland games that introduced me to Piobaireachd. This particular games was in Auckland, New Zealand; Mount Eden I think. After having performed a not particularly successful rendition of Highland Wedding, my pipe major and a couple of band members consoled me by taking me off to sit in a small concert hall to listen to the Piobaireachd competition. I was totally awestruck right from note one. My piping colleagues explained to me that Piobaireachd is the oldest forms of bagpipe music, composed by the ancients from 1700s and beyond. It is still being composed today, but it is the ancient pieces that mark out this genre of music. (Incidentally Mackintosh's Lament dates from the very early 1500s.) They told me how it was a form of improvised music where the piper has a kind of grounding of what to play at the core and a framework from which to improvise. They told me how there can be a special set of grace notes just used in Piobaireachd. How the music is always played slowly but that the art of a good Piobaireachd player is to play just slow enough to create an atmosphere but not so slowly that the energy is taken out of the music. So there you go, I am being rather cowardly and relating to you what my piping colleagues told me about Piobaireachd all those years ago in Mount Eden, New Zealand; that way if I'm wrong in what I tell you, dear reader, well we can all blame them. I can however speak from my experience and say that Piobaireachd moved me that day. I absolutely loved the slow emotive resonant sounds of the music. Have a listen to Mackintosh's Lament and see if it moves you too.

9 August: Cumha Mhic Shimidh (or Lord Lovat's Lament)

Composer: Piobaireachd - Ancient

We're on a roll now. Having finally mustered up the courage to write about Piobaireachd yesterday, I am just going to keep going because I love it so much and I'm hoping to bring you along on that journey of appreciation. Also there was something that I only briefly mentioned yesterday that I thought would be worth expanding on, namely that this is the music of the ancients. Both of Cumha Mhic Shimidh and Cumha Mhic an Toisich appear in the book 'A Collection of Ancient Piobaireachd', in which it states that Cumha Mhic Shimidh dates from 1746 and Cumha Mhic an Toisich dates from "about the year" 1526.

I guess that you may not have as instant a reaction to Piobaireachd as I did when I first heard it so I thought that we could take the music and travel back in time as a way to appreciate it. In the first instance though I can recommend taking yourself off to a forest or a mountain or hill in the area where you live and be at peace and then listen to it. Let the music just wash over you, don't try to understand it. Just let it be there, as you are, in this presence of nature. Then let's go back in time, through Scottish history and tune our ears in to this music of the ancients. This was the very music that surrounded the air of those ancient clansmen. It filled the mist covered mountains and swirled about the castle walls. Not the castle walls of the derelict versions that we see today, but instead the castle walls with hanging tapestries and roaring fires and Scottish lairds ruling over their clan. Can you smell the wild boar from the recent hunt roasting on the fire yet?

Backwards we go until we land in 1746 and Cumha Mhic Shimidh. One year before on the 16 April 1745 the bloody battle of Culloden had been fought. Bonnie Prince Charlie had raised the Scots clans to fight against the English and had almost succeeded if not for a

Julia Read

somewhat foolhardy retreat that led finally to one of the bloodiest battles at Culloden moor. It took one day for the English to mow down the Scots and force them into submission. After this victory the English started on a period of wiping out the Clan heritage. The wearing of tartan was banned, the speaking of Gaelic was banned. It would have been in this environment of fighting for the survival of a culture that Cumha Mhic Shimidh was written.

Shall we carry on backwards through time? Here we go then. Back through Scotland of the 1600s when clan life was thriving. Back to 1526 when Cumha Mhic an Toisich makes its appearance. Henry VIII is ruler of England and the boy king, James V, came to power in Scotland; April 1526 at the age of 14 to be precise. You can read all about the history of James V, of how he was kidnapped for 3 years by a power hungry step father and then finally escaped in 1528 to begin ruling without the influence of others. However I think that we ought to take a look into the life of the ordinary folk as we listen to Cumha Mhic an Toisich. By all accounts James V was quite concerned with their lot because he used to travel anonymously around the country in disguise, perhaps as a way of understanding their needs better. So what was life like for the ordinary Scottish folk when Cumha Mhic an Toisich filled the air? We can get some idea if we go back to Pitlochry (27 April) and drive 20 miles down the road to Loch Tay. That is where the Scottish Crannog Centre is located. You can look it up online and you will see the fully restored Crannog, which is a round house built from wood with a coned thatched roof, under the apex of which was a fire for cooking and warmth. This particular Crannog is built on a pier just off the shores of Loch Tay. May I suggest that you take a look for yourself and read all about life in this time. Play Cumha Mhic an Toisich, relax and just breathe it all in.

12 August: Little Bird

Composer: Annie Lennox

I'd like you to imagine one of those graphic animations where you are way out in space. Then you start zooming into the Earth. Down and down until the Earth is no longer a globe but you are now focussed on the Northern Hemisphere. Keep going, there's Europe, closer yet to the United Kingdom, keep zooming in. Now we could zoom in to Aberdeen, afterall that is where Annie Lennox comes from. But don't get diverted. Refocus that zoom and swerve down from Aberdeen to London, East London to be precise and the Olympic Stadium. Down we go, through the open roof of the stadium and here we have arrived at the closing night of the London Olympics on 12 August 2012.

Annie Lennox is wheeled in at the helm of an enormous wooden boat whilst a dance troupe of a hundred or so men and women

dressed in flamboyant neoclassical 18th century garments parade beneath her, emulating the waves of the sea that Annie's boat is forging through, whilst she performs her song 'Little Bird'. This is a woman whose final year school report from the Royal Academy of Music stated that she didn't always know where she was going. Personally I love it. I love the transformation from talented but directionless music student, to determined and forthright Diva.

Finding one's purpose in life isn't easy. Sometimes we never really get there. I'm not sure that all of us have to arrive on a large wooden boat and give one of the greatest performances of the universe. We are probably not capable of it, let's be honest. I can speak only of my own experience and from that I can relate to what Annie says in her song 'Little Bird', a feeling all my life of 'being blessed' and that despite the troubles that I may have had there was somehow this guiding light, something looking after me. Let's test these wings out then, shall we?

Julia Read

18 August: Hearts of Olden Glory

Composer: Rory Macdonald / Calum Macdonald

Stirling castle, 18 August 2018. Fireworks exploding illuminating Stirling castle, a light drizzle in the air, people hugging and lamenting the passing of a 45 year run. Need I say more?

19 August: The Bonnie Banks of Loch Lomond

Composer: Traditional - unknown

Ok if you have no idea what yesterday's entry was all about, may I please point you to the band Runrig. I am not going to say any more about the band as I don't know enough about them. However I do know how much affection many Scots have for the band. Not just Scots. That final tour in 2018 went all round Europe.

But the reason for referencing Runrig here in relation to 'The Bonnie Banks of Loch Lomond' is that they made it their own. They sang it at the end of every concert apparently (apart from that last concert it seems, when 'Hearts of Olden Glory' was the last song). As one commenter on a well known streaming site put it, words to the effect of …

"til you've been at a wedding or pub at the end of a night, belting out The Bonnie Banks surrounded by a band of happy and drunken Scots, you've not lived"

I don't feel there is much more to say about the song. No-one seems to know who wrote it, but everyone knows it. If you are fan of Scotland, which afterall must be why you are reading this book, you surely already know this song and if you don't, well, then I'm speechless. If you don't know Runrig's version (I'm ashamed to say that I didn't) check it out, it's fab.

21 August: My Love She's But a Lassie Yet

Composer: Words – Robert Burns, Tune - traditional

There are many stories about the creativity that managed to survive during both World Wars. Olivier Messiaen's composition of 'Quatuour pour la fin du temps' for example was written during the winter of 1940 whilst Messiaen was interned in a German Stalag camp near Dresden. That same winter and 400 miles south, in Laufen castle Bavaria, the Scottish soldiers of the 51st Highland Division were also being creative; in this case coming up with a new Scottish Country Dance. The Reel of the 51st Division nowadays is most commonly danced to the tune 'The Drunken Piper', but when it was originally conceived in that German Oflag it was put to the tune of 'My Love She's But a Lassie Yet'[10]. Lt Jimmy Atkinson had the original idea for the dance as a way to keep his mind on more positive thoughts during the long trudge through Holland as a PoW that he and his comrades had to make after being captured due to the Dunkirk "incident". The idea was to represent the Highland Division's sign of the St. Andrew's Cross in a dance. The dance was first performed for the 51st Division's commander, Major-General Victor Fortune KBE, who stayed interned with his men despite suffering a stroke in 1944 and refusing to be sent home. It is in tribute to Major-General Fortune KBE that makes me tell this story on this date of his birth, namely 21 August 1883. We can perhaps imagine being Major-General Fortune KBE, the first audience of this dancing creation, and listen to 'My Love She's But a Lassie Yet' whilst we imagine the men of the 51st Highland Division dancing their new Reel in front of us.

Incidentally, the Division even managed to send the dance home to Scotland, despite the Germans intercepting it and trying to decode it for hidden messages. A friend of mine, namely Patricia Reid of The Reid Scottish Dancers, related to me how her mother was part of the dance troupe that put on its first performance in Perthshire – the Royal Scottish Country Dance Society. It is due to Pat that I know of this story. So thank you Pat and thank you Lt

Jimmy Atkinson et al for the Reel of the 51st Highland Division, one of the most popular of the Scottish country dance canon.

23 August: A Girl Like You

Composer: Edwyn Collins

A musical friend of mine commented that "Edwyn Collins musical influence can be seen across most good Scottish indie music". If you look at the comments posted on videos for 'A Girl Like You', you will see that many agree that his music is exceptional. Commenters refer to this as the perfect killer song, saying that Collins is a hero for writing a song with methaphorically and allegorically in the lyrics and for their useage to actually make sense. Writing a song with only 1 chord yet with all other harmony simply being implied. The praise goes on.

Written and performed by Edinburgh born singer-songwriter Edwyn Collins (born 23 August 1959), 'A Girl Like You' is a great song to bring into your summer. Last bar-b-q of the season maybe? Put this one on and bop around while reminiscing about all that great music from the 90s.

24 August: Waverley Steps

Composer: Fish

The same musical friend who from yesterday told me that Edwyn Collins is the father of modern Scottish indie music, also suggested that I include Waverley Steps in this book. The date of 24 August has no significance (not that I'm aware of!), the track is merely included here to link up these two suggestions by my friend. You know, sometimes, finding significant dates for a book like this can be hard – I'm sure that you will give me a break and allow this tenuous link.

Anyway, Waverley Steps by Fish. What can I tell you? Are you familiar with Prog Rock already? Yes? Then you are going to know so much about Fish already, you can skip everything I'm about to say and just go ahead and listen to this 13min epic one more glorious time.

If you don't know who Fish is, or rather Derek William Dick as he was named at birth (25 April 1958, in Edinburgh, grew up in Dalkeith – just saying!), and from the above paragraph you've not already guessed that he is one of the most acclaimed Prog Rockers in the world, then let me introduce you to him. Ex lead singer of the band Marillion, acclaimed to be a genius lyricist. In fact my musical friend and I were out on a walk and I said that I would like to include 'Grace of God' into this book as a Fish track but I was having trouble with the lyrics cos they were a bit dark and I couldn't quite understand them. What followed was a 40 minute "explanation" on the genius of Fish's lyrics and that the tune that I should really recommend is Waverley Steps because the meanings of the words are so nuanced and multi-dimensional that it is just simply a work of art. Oh and another thing ….. [40 minutes!] …..

We finished that walk, my friend and I. We took off our boots and I came upstairs and dialled up Waverley Steps. Yes, I quite agree with him. You have to hear it! It will only take 13 minutes, but that is just the first time. There will be all those other 13 minutes when you listen to it again and again.

SEPTEMBER

1 September: God Most High

Composer: David Lyon

Try typing 'the satellite project scotland' into an online search engine and the results might just surprise you. The Scottish space industry is alive and thriving it seems. A rocket launch pad is due to go live in 2023 or so, in the a' Mhoine peninsula, allowing 12 launches a year. Plus there are numerous other results documenting the thriving Scottish satellite industry. But this is not the Satellite Project that we are after here, ours is more Godly. Take that search term and then add 'christian music' to it and you will then land on the initiative that Scottish musician and composer David Lyon set up in 2010. A collective of Scottish musicians writing modern and contemporary hymns. That is where we want to be for today's entry – Christian music that is modern and contemporary and comes from a host of talented Scottish composers.

'God Most High' is based on the message in Psalm 27; God as our saviour. The recording of 'God Most High' from the album 'Faithful' includes a celtic sounding flute, guitar and the beautiful voice of Yvonne Lyon. Dial this one up on your smart phone, headphones on and pop outside into that glorious world. Thanks be for all of this.

Julia Read

20 September: Ali Bali Bee

Composer: Robert Coltard

Is Galashiels the home of Scottish fabric design and manufacturer? Robert Coltard certainly thought so when he moved there in the 1840s as a young man from Galloway to train as a weaver. The world famous Heriot-Watt university certainly seemed to think so when in 1998 they completed a full merger with the Scottish College of Textiles, (previously founded by the Scottish Woollen Manufacturers Association in the 1900s), to create the Scottish Borders campus: School of Textiles and Design in Galashiels. The first mills were set up in Galashiels in 1800 by the Manufacturer's Corporation of Galashiels, having begun linen production in the area in 1777. But the history of weaving in the area goes further back than that, all the way to the middle ages in fact.

What must it have felt like for the teenager Robert Coltard to set out from his birthplace in Galloway and arrive at Galashiels in the 1840s? He would have travelled past Sir Walter Scott's home, Abbotsford, on the banks of the river Tweed and was probably bursting with the enthusiasm of youth for this new life and job ahead of him. It was obviously a bit of a financial struggle this weaving career because Robert took to making boiled sweets as a way to supplement his income. Five miles down the road from Galashiels in Melrose, Robert become a sweet maker. This is where his contribution to the Scottish music catalogue comes in.

A simple little ditty 'Ali Bali Bee'. Robert wrote it and sang it as a way to announce his arrival to all the children in the area to bring their money out and buy his sweets. 'Ali Bali Bee', sometimes referred to a 'Coulter's candy' caught on as a nursery rhyme for parents to sing to their wee bairns while rocking them to sleep. Parents have passed the song down through the generations and so it has survived long after Robert's untimely death in 1880[11] at the age of only 48. It gained a wider audience in the 1960s when it was recorded as a folk tune by Robin Hall and Jimmie MacGregor.

Maybe Robert goes to show that a side gig, especially one that is creative and entrepreneurial, is a way to leave a legacy to the world. His song is still sung today and on 20 September 2019 a statue of Robert, selling his candy, was unveiled in Galashiels town centre. It was completed in December that year by the addition of two further bronzes of a young boy, little Jock, and a young girl, wee Jeannie.

So, if you are heading off to Scotland, please don't just drive through the border country on your way to the Highlands. Why not take a trip to Galashiels and do the town trail – Robert, little Jock and wee Jeannie are waiting to welcome you to their town, the history of this area and the lush scenery of the rivers, forests and hillsides that make up the Scottish Borders.

22 September: An Old Friend

Composer: Fergus McCreadie

The Scottish jazz festival year is kicked off by Aberdeen in March, followed by the Edinburgh jazz festival in July, via Islay and right through to the Glasgow jazz festival in Nov/Dec. The Fergus McCreadie trio are very much a part of this thriving Scottish jazz scene. Fergus graduated from the Royal Conservatoire of Scotland in 2018 with a BMus where he studied jazz and composition. He has won a number of awards including twice winning the Young Scottish Jazz Musician of the year and his trio won the presitigious Peter Whittingham Jazz Award in 2016.

This composition by Fergus, "An Old Friend", is so gentle and moving. There are two versions that I can recommend that you search out. The first is recorded 'Live in Glasgow'. In this version the trio play the head (the thematic melody) without any improvisation. This is sweet and pensive and Fergus uses a simple rocking in the left hand on the piano all the way through the piece. This rocking underpins the melody like a simple but steady foundation. To me, this seems like a wonderful representation of the stability and reliability of the song's title subject "An Old Friend".

The second version that I can recommend is the nine minute version published by The Orchard Enterprises. This starts off with the head, sweetly and gently as before but then the trio improvise away and the tension builds. Fergus's left hand piano turns from a gentle rocking to a faster paced boiling roll and Stephen Henderson on drums brings in clashing symbols which just adds to the tension. In the last few minutes however, the trio return to the sweet peacefulness of the head and the simple rocking of the left hand on the piano. Call me an old sentimentalist but I just love how this dynamic represents the role that those old friends so often play in our lives. We start off in the spring of our life, full of vigour and youth and along the way we find these special people that will stay our friends forever. As life carries us on into the summer we so often face struggles, just the struggles of life sometimes, like the pressures of kids, paying a mortgage and trying to get a promotion at work. Then our life moves into our autumn, into our September, and the struggles subside and we slide into the start of retirement. The world calms and just like the sweet peaceful ending of this rendition of "An Old Friend", we find that those true friends that we made at the start of our lives are still there. Dependable, reliable and beautiful, just as 'An Old Friend'.

26 September: Downton Abbey Theme Music

Composer: John Lunn

I have rather reluctantly put this entry here on 26 September. It was the date in 2010 that Downton Abbey first aired, having its first showing on ITV in the UK. My reluctance is due to not wanting to typecast Stirling born composer John Lunn with the Downton Abbey theme music. Lunn is an Emmy Award winning composer who has written an incredibly diverse array of music, not only for TV dramas such as Little Dorrit, The White Queen and Shetland, but he has also composed several operas. So associating him only with Downton Abbey does seem a tad unfair.

In an interview with Kay Hutchison on the Bellemedia.co.uk Belle Books and Stories podcast, Lunn gives a fascinating insight into the process of composing for TV dramas. The main theme for Downton Abbey for example was created by John repeatedly looking at the opening scenes of episode 1 which showed a telegraph operator signalling in the news of the Titanic and a worried man on a train (which turned out to be Mr Bates travelling to Downton Abbey to take up his post as a valet despite his dodgy leg). John Lunn composed the theme music based on these first scenes and points out that that first episode didn't have any opening credits. It was only later that the producers created opening credits, but rather unusually they did this by fitting clips to the music that John had composed rather than create the clips and have the composer create from that. As John rather amusingly remarks to Kay, if he'd been given the images of those opening credits (which starts with a view of a dog's bum!), then he is not sure that he would have come up with the same theme music. With this insight, I am going to suggest that you go back and watch season 1 episode 1 and compare it with the opening credits of other episodes. I say 'go back' of course because I am assuming that you've already seen the show. If not, well, what is there to say, you really must! Whether you watch it all again, or for the first time, keep that ear out for Lunn's music. He spent 6 months of every year during the show's production working on its music. Enjoy!

OCTOBER

2 October: 故郷の空

Composer: Lyrics – Robert Burns, Music - unknown

The mid 1800s to the early part of the 20th Century, are known as the Meiji era in Japan and they mark the first half of what is called the Empire of Japan. A great wave of Western scientific, technological, political, legal, artistic and philosophical ideas surged into the country and influenced the transformation from a feudal society to the modern industrialised nation state and great power of today. Surf boarding in on the crest of this wave were a clan of Scottish folk songs. Having landed ashore, they picked up their boards, walked inland and rooted themselves firmly and squarely into Japanese culture. 故郷の空 is one such tune; 'Hometown Sky' being the English translation, although if you are Scottish you will recognise the melody as that of 'Coming Through the Rye'.

As is typical of Robert Burns, his lyrics for 'Coming Through the Rye' are rather bawdy and tell of "love" in a wheat field; so bawdy in fact that the BBC banned the song in the 1950s! Maybe the Japanese thought so too because they transformed the lyrics into a more nostalgic, wistful song about one's hometown. I have read that it is easier for Japanese people to say 'that melody flowing on the pedestrian crossing' than 'Hometown Sky', which might explain why you will hear 'Coming Through the Rye' played at pedestrian crossings in Japan. Try the search term 'Nagano Comin' thro the Rye' if you don't believe me.

After the war, the lyrics for 'Hometown Sky' were adapted to be more akin to the Robert Burns lyrics. Well at least in as much as they now reference a wheat field that is true. The bawdiness of Burns has been toned down and it is now a more appropriately wholesome walk of two people through a wheat field. 麦畑 (Barley field) is how the song is now known in Japan and is sung in most elementary schools. The Japanese NHK drama 'Massan' features both the Scottish version and 'Hometown Sky' within the narrative. It is the story of a Scottish lass (Ellie) marrying her Japanese hero (Masahura), returning home to Japan to start up the Nikka Whisky distillery. It is based on a true story and as a result of the success of the show, sales in Nikka Whisky soared.

Like many countries around the world Japan has incorporated the Scottish traditions of whisky, folk songs and bagpipes into her culture and made them her own. The Japan Highland Games has been held every year in Chiba university, Tokyo since the 1980s and tartan is a common feature in Japan's school uniforms for example. Maybe the awareness of where these things came from has eroded into the past, but they are still very much a part of the culture of Japan today.

Oh and if you are wondering what other Scottish folk song surf boarded its way into Japan during the Meiji era, try visiting Japan's shops at closing time and you might well hear 蛍の光 (Firefly Light), or as the Scottish know it – Auld Lang Syne.

14 October: Wings

Composer: William Newstead

'Wings' is a bagpipe tune, ok! It is! It is a bagpiping tune! Oh, ok then I suppose if I had to be totally accurate William Newstead did sort of write it as a brass band arrangement. Newstead (b. 1826) was the Bandmaster of the Royal Engineer Establishment. He created 'Wings' by arranging a variety of other historic tunes from England and Germany. So we've got a tune that was originally composed for brass bands, written by a Brit and pulled together from English and German tunes. So, what, I hear you ask, is it doing in here, a book on music composed by Scots? I can't think of a viable excuse for you, other than it is a bloomin bagpipe tune, ok?!!! Well, me and my bagpiping mates play it and most every piper that I know plays it, plus if you are piper in America then you'll find it on the EUSPBA[12] list of approved (ie read popular) tunes for massed bands. So, I'm very sorry, but it is staying in.

Now we've got that out of the way, what about the tune and why is it in here for 14 October? Well let's take that date aspect first. 14 October is the date of a letter that Lord Kitchener wrote re-instating 'Wings' as the official march of the Royal Engineers. He'd previously had extensive conversation with the War office to get them to approve this decision. Why had he done this? Well, after Bandmaster William Newstead composed 'Wings' and the Royal Engineers used it for many years on official marches and standing out on parade, it seems that the Commander-in-Chief of the corps decided it was too frivolous and banned it. Lord Kitchener had been familiar with the tune from his younger military days and when he came back from the Boer war in 1902 was dismayed to find that they no longer used it. So, he got in touch with the War office and eventually that letter was written, reinstating Wings as the official march of the Royal Engineers.

It is a cracking tune, so it is no surprise that it was transcribed for pipe bands. They've been playing it since before WWI and so it is most definitely a stalwart of the piping repertoire. You will very often hear it played as a medley with Scotland the Brave. In fact if you are in America and a pipe band marches past you playing Scotland the Brave, I'm going to go out on a limb here and suggest that the tune they follow on with will be Wings. If you are learning the pipes, dig out the music for Wings and learn it right now. You won't regret it.

27 October: Culloden Moor Suite: March

Composer: Bobby Wellins

If you had been serving with PM Jim Riddell (13 June) in the Falklands war (1982) then in order to communicate orders amongst the troops you may well have been trying out an early prototype of the Ptarmigan[13] mobile radio system. But go back a couple of hundred years to the battle of Culloden and the only 'mobile radio' systems available then were the drum corps. Each infantry battalion had a corps of drums because it was about the only thing that could cut through the noise of the battle. A mass of drummers would ring out specific signals using the patterns that they created and this would have been very much the predominant sound coming from the British side at the battle of Culloden. The Scottish Jacobites of course would have been sounding the pipes. Imagine yourself as a bystander at that battle. Let's put you in a specially constructed tower so that you are nice and safely tucked away from all the blood letting. Now close your eyes and listen. What you will hear, amongst the canon fire and full rage of battle, will be the pipes slowly being extinguished whilst the drummers get louder and louder, until finally there is a deathly quiet. Gun smoke fills your nostrils and you know that the slaughter is complete. The final sounds that you heard had come from the 200 or so drummers of the British army as they marched to victory.

Open your eyes. Let's get you out of there. Back to this lovely day in October in the 21st century, all safe and sound and not a canon in sight. Now take a listen to the Glaswegian Saxophonist Jazz legend Bobby Wellins[14] and his composition Culloden Moor Suite: March. There are 5 parts to the suite: Gathering, March, Battle, Aftermath, Epilogue. You are listening to 'March', ie the bit before the battle. Which side do you think this music represents, the Jacobites or the British? The first quarter has the Scottish National Jazz Orchestra full of confident sway and swagger – there is even a shout! Then Wellins comes in for his solo and plays in his very characteristic style. This is the usual improvisation that a jazz piece takes – play the head first, then instruments solo over the chord progression. Perhaps this typical structure symbolises the usual processes that an army goes through before battle? The mood is frenetic with lots of activity, perhaps that is also the activity of an army before battle? But then we get to 8:45 minutes in and the mood changes. This tribe of people that have accompanied the music up to the 8:45 minute point, they were on a sway and swagger of a march. They were carrying out their typical activities in a frenetic but structured way. But at 8:45 minutes, we encounter the drummers. These are not the drummers of a roaring Jacobite army. These are military precision drummers, perhaps those of the British army? But that doesn't seem to phase that tribe that got us to the 8:45 minute mark because at 9:40 they return to their swagger and sway. The battle hasn't happened yet. There is still hope.

Julia Read

30 October: Assassins
Creed III: any track

Composer: Lorne Balfe

It is late October and you have decided to take your family on a late holiday to the Highlands of Scotland. Arriving at Glasgow International airport, you pick up your hire car, pack all of your luggage into the boot and set off. It isn't long before the cityscape of Glasgow is behind you and the lush green forests of Loch Lomond surround. Your destination? A log cabin at the foothills of Ben Nevis in Banavie, near Fort William. For miles and miles (27miles in fact), it seems that the wonder of Loch Lomond will never end. You drive along its western side and your family gape in awe at the beauty of this place.

As you keep driving the A82, the forests start to disappear until eventually you hit the purple heather glazed moors that precede Glen Coe. In the windscreen you see the mighty sight of the mountains of Glen Coe and turn round to make sure that your kids are taking this all in – they aren't, they are asleep on the back seat, tired from the long flight. 'Ah well, they'll see it tomorrow', you say to your spouse, 'when we come back this way to visit Inveraray castle'; onward you drive. The mountains of Glencoe engulf your little car and weave you through valley after valley until suddenly you emerge at Loch Leven. Through the steel trusses of Ballachulish bridge you drive. Two hours you've been driving. It has been a glorious drive through spectacular scenery, and it turns out that the remaining 20 minutes to Fort William are just as spectacular as you cover the coast road. The ferries and fishing boats skim in front of distant mountains of the Morvern peninsula, sailing purposely through the sea water of Loch Linnhe.

The kids wake up just as you drive over Neptune's Staircase and you are soon pulling into the log cabin, checking in, unloading and putting the kettle on for a little refresher before you head out tonight. Oh, did I not mention? You have bought the family an evening out. Tickets to the Fort William Accordion and Fiddle club to go and see some real live Scottish music. Just time for a quick shower and you'll be ready to soak up some good ole Scottish culture.

Refreshed and with towel wrapped round your torso, you emerge from the bathroom only to find that the kids have discovered that the host of the log cabin has included an Xbox 360 along with the TV. They are delighted, and engrossed! Here then is your challenge. You must make a decision. Do you stay in with the kids and play Assassins Creed III or unplug the Xbox and insist everyone joins you at the fiddle club? Which of your options gives you the best chance of fulfilling your quest to experience Scottish music this evening?

Well, it turns out that whichever option you go for, then you are going to experience Scottish music because the entire sound track of Assassins Creed III was written by the Scottish games/film/tv composer Lorne Balfe. He grew up in Edinburgh, studied music at school and headed off to LA to study film composing with the greats. He collaborated with Danish composer Jesper Kyd for previous Assassins Creed soundtracks, but III was all entirely the work of Balfe.

Balfe's work is prodigious. Look him up on Wikipedia and you will be skimming page after page of listings of his compositions. But he isn't the only Scottish composer writing music for games. There are many others. So, if it is music composed by Scots that you are after, don't overlook your kid's computer games. Scotland might be closer than you think.

NOVEMBER

3 November: I Don't Wanna Fight

Composer: Lulu

Chances are, if you know this pop song, you will know it because of the Tina Turner version. Turner hit the charts with 'I Don't Wanna Fight' in 1993 when she incorporated it into her autobiographical film What's Love Got to Do With It. But it was Scottish singer Lulu that actually wrote the song (along with her brother Billy Lawrie and British composer Steve DuBarry).

Lulu was born in Stirlingshire on 3 November 1948 and her family soon moved to Glasgow, where she grew up. She came to fame in the 60s with a rock raw powerful voice in songs like Shout and To Sir With Love which reached No. 1 in the United States.

If you haven't heard the Lulu version of 'I Don't Wanna Fight', then I can recommend that you search out two performances that were given decades apart. The first is from the UK news/magazine program 'Pebble Mill' and the second is from the UK show 'The Gloria Hunniford Show'. Lulu's version of her song is much more toned down in volume than Tina Turner's. Tina belts it out as a power ballad and as such its mood is predominantly defiant; the sort of song that might convince one to leave an abusive relationship. Lulu's version in contrast is subtle and wistful. This creates a more reflective regretful mood. Both versions work. I personally prefer Lulu's version and find it interesting to hear an extra dimension of wisdom and maturity added to the version in the Gloria Hunniford Show compared to the earlier Pebble Mill version. Both are quietly reflective, but the latter version really injects an incredible amount of compassion into the lyrics. It is a version of tolerance and kindness, of regret yet an unflinching acceptance that there is no going back. Coupled with the beautifully tonal quality of Lulu's voice and her incredible control and ability to vocally nuance the melody, it truly is a beautiful beautiful thing. Much like Lulu herself! A beautiful, powerful, Scottish lass.

5 November: The Land of the Mountain and the Flood

Composer: Hamish MacCunn

This is one of those classical pieces of music that you might well have heard many times before but don't know the title of. Well here it is. A classical overture for orchestra, composed by the Scottish Hamish MacCunn in 1887 and first performed on 5 November of the same year – Crystal Palace was the location of this first performance apparently. By various accounts, this first performance got a rather negative review from George Bernard Shaw – his review is documented online so there is no need to repeat it here. However, what I'd like to note is that despite this negative review Hamish didn't let it affect him it seems as he continued to compose music year on year, pretty much every year thereafter. Quite right too! Just because someone has a negative opinion of a creative piece of work, that shouldn't stop anyone continuing to create in my opinion. Besides, this particular piece is lovely and many others seem to think so too as it has lasted the test of time, it is widely performed by orchestras and became familiar in the 1970s when it was used as a TV theme tune. Yes indeedy Mr Shaw, The Land of the Mountain and the Flood is wonderful and I am most certainly not alone in being grateful that Hamish MacCunn created it.

11 November: Flowers of the Forest

Composer: Words – Jean Elliot

The 'Flowers of the Forest' was the name given to the archers of Ettrick Forest[15] when they fought alongside William Wallace (Braveheart from 3 January) during the battle of Falkirk in 1298. The epithet stayed with them through the years and they came to be the bodyguard of the Kings of Scotland. In 1513 they fought alongside King James IV in the disastrous battle of Flodden. A bloody battle that saw the slaughter of many of King James's nobles as well as the archers and King James IV himself; the last Monarch from Great Britain to die in battle. Casualty numbers vary, a contemporary account puts it at 10,000 men, King Henry VIII issued a report that 12,000 Scots were killed. By any account it was a large number and led to the name of the Ettrick archers being extended to all of those fallen Scots in 1513. So significant an event is it in Scottish history that it is possible to visit Flodden and see the stone cross that was erected in memory of King James IV and his men.

Two hundred and forty years after this event, in 1756, Scottish poet Jean Elliot penned her lyrics. She put these to an earlier Aire (tune) that originated from the early 1600s which had been entitled Flowres of the Forrest and then published this song anonymously. This led to a belief that the song was a surviving ancient ballad but Robert Burns and Sir Walter Scott suspected it as being a contemporary composition and managed to reveal that it was indeed Jean Elliot that wrote it.

Jean Elliot's words speak of the women and children left behind when their men did not return from battle. She talks of the women and bairns in the meadows, milking the cows, no longer lilting, but instead full of grief that the 'flowers of the forest' had all withered away. It is a very powerful lament and poignant song, spoken from a woman's perspective of the experience of war. As such, it has passed down through the years and is oft played on days of remembrance, such as we have today on 11 November. The Scottish singer Isla St Clair has sung it on a number of occasions I believe and it is well worth searching out her rendition. It is also incredible powerful when played on the bagpipes and is very often played by pipers at funerals and memorials.

There is one further place where you might hear The Flowers of the Forest; this time played as both a march and as a lament. That is at the Common Ridings that take place in the borders of Scotland every year. These go back at least 400 years and are actually thought to date back to those battles from 1513. It is said that a lone standard bearer returned to Selkirk from the battle of Flodden and dropped a British flag in the town square; this was sadly the sign that all had fallen and he was the only survivor. The Selkirk Common Ridings sees 300 – 400 horsemen race out of the town each year symbolising the checking of the Scottish/English borders. It is apparently the largest cavalcade of horses and riders in Europe.

Whichever experience of the Flowers of the Forest you search out, at a memorial service, at a funeral or at the Selkirk Common Ridings, I hope that you agree with me that it is a very fitting lament to remember those who are sadly no longer with us.

14 November: Fingal's Cave

Composer: Felix Mendelssohn

Felix Mendelssohn penned Fingal's cave whilst on a visit to Scotland. He wasn't Scottish himself so is it fair to claim this piece of music as a Creation of Scotland? I think so. The work was inspired by a creation of Scotland's afterall, namely its geography.

Mendelssohn was 20 when he wrote his Hebridean overture (known as Fingal's Cave). Apparently the first few phrases of the tune came to him as he was rounding the island by boat. When he got back to his lodgings he convinced his hosts to let him use the piano; it was a sabbath so he had a bit of convincing to do! There and then he played those first few musical phrases and worked on the overture, so that it was completed in 1830 and published 2 years later.

I have seen the Isle of Staffa on a calm day when the crystal clear waters surrounded it like a giant mirror and I have seen it in weather that might make a seasoned fisherman head for home. My guess is that Mendelsohn visited on a rough weather day with sea swells and crashing waves against the basalt rock formations. The Hebrides Op26 (Fingal's Cave) overture certainly represents a scene of sea swells and crashing waves. Moments of peace hang in the air, with small little florets of musical motifs that could well represent the Puffins and Black Guillemots that bob and duck and dive around the island. This peace builds into multiple crescendos, much like a small boat leaving the docking bay on Staffa and rounding the hexagonal rock forms out into the open sea. Waves rolling in, spray flying against the rocky island and a great torrent of Atlantic sea water rushing in and out of the narrow Fingal's cave. All of that potential energy being turned into kinetic. That rolling, surging energy is contrastingly caught in the sweetness as well as the power of Mendelssohn's composition.

The only other thing that I'd like to say about this Mendelssohn composition is to explain why I have placed it on 14 November. 14th November was the birth date of Felix's sister, Fanny. 1805 to be precise. It seems that Fanny was as prolific and skilful a composer as Felix, but because of the era in which she lived, she was never able to publish her work. Her brother published much of her work (as well as his own) under the monica of F. Mendelssohn. Musical historians are still going through the process of revealing which of F. Mendelssohn's compositions belong to Fanny and which belong to Felix. So in this my dedication to Felix Mendelssohn for Fingal's cave, I feel that I'd also like to pay tribute to Fanny as well. So here we have a celebration of both the Mendelssohn siblings. They may not have both created music in dedication to the wonder that is Scotland, but it seems only fair to pay tribute to them both, here on this day.

15 November: Sea Plaint (Osnadh na Mara), Op. 14 No. 4

Composer: Julian Nesbitt

Yesterday we had a German composing music for the Hebrides and I snuck him in on the basis that his composition was about a Scottish Creation (its geography). Today we are going to have an actual Scottish born composer and the music that he composed for the Hebrides, namely Julian Nesbitt. 'From Hebrid Seas' (also known as the Celtic Suite) consists of 4 movements and for today

I'm going to recommend that you listen to the 4th movement, 'Sea Plaint'. It was written for the organ and Nesbitt performed it on the organ, but it has been arranged for the piano. You could search out someone like Phillip Sear for example to hear a beautiful rendition of it expressively played on the piano.

Julian Nesbitt was born right on the border between Scotland and England, in the town of Coldstream. Being in the Scottish borders, he would have been very familiar with the Common Ridings that took place every year[16]. Historically this was a way to check that the Scottish borders were still safe, but in Nesbitt's time, as today, these are symbolic and ceremonial.

Nesbitt was born in 1877 and died in 1927. In his life he took up a number of instruments including flute, organ, violin, piano and a number of brass instruments. All of this despite losing his little finger on his left hand when he was a child. He became a bandmaster at the age of 15, so he really was a bit of child musical prodigy. Later in life he moved out to the West of Scotland (Oban) and became inspired by the Hebrides, it's culture and musical heritage.

If you liked listening to 'Sea Plaint' then I think that you will also like a couple of his other Hebridean inspired compositions. Hebridean Sketches Op. 10 and Idylls of Iona Op. 16. It might take a bit of hunting down, but well worth it in my opinion.

27 November: You & I

Composer: Alec Dalglish (Skerryvore)

If you like Runrig (see 18, 19 August) then I feel sure that you will like this track and the band Skerryvore. Skerryvore are a celtic rock band from Tiree, Argyll and Bute. They have a lineup that includes traditional instruments like fiddle, accordion, celtic flute and 2 bagpipers as well as rock guitars and drums. You will hear the diversity of the band if you listen to this song 'You & I' and compare it with another offering 'Soraidh Slan' composed by one of the 4 founding band members Martin Gillespie. 'You & I', composed by lead singer Alec Dalglish, is a rock anthem that you could imagine dancing to at the end of a gig, hands pumping in the sky. In contrast 'Soraidh Slan' is very ethereal and celtic sounding.

In 2020 Skerryvore won the award for Original Work of the Year[17] for their composition 'Everyday Heroes'. It was written to raise funds for NHS and emergency services workers during the 2020 Covid pandemic and reached No. 1 in the charts. This, along with 'You & I' and 'Soraidh Slan', is yet another one of Skerryvore's tracks that it is worth searching out and listening to.

The band have been going since 2005, so that is 15 years at the time of writing this book. If you haven't heard of them yet, then they are definitely one to check out. But do it quick because Ken Bruce has started playing 'You & I' on BBC Radio 2. So, if you want to claim to be there before they were world globally mega famous, you had better open up that search engine and type in 'Skerryvore'.

30 November: Flower of Scotland

Composer: Roy Williamson

1990 was quite a year for the boys of the Pipes and Drums of the Queen Victoria School, Dunblane. In August they played at the Edinburgh Tattoo, but that is a frequent occurrence for the band so it wasn't that that was memorable. No, the event that probably stays with those young men right up to this day was that they were the pipe band that played the Flower of Scotland at Murray Field at that famous match Scotland v England Five Nations Rugby 1990. It was the decider match for the grand slam and Scotland trounced it with a 13 – 7 victory; as such it has gone down in Rugby history in Scotland and the opening rendition of Flower of Scotland that was sung so passionately by the players and played so well by the QV Pipe band became almost a national anthem for Scotland. Every Scot surely knows it. You will certainly hear it being sung today because today is St. Andrews day, the national saints day for Scotland.

The song was written by Edinburgh born Roy Williamson (from The Corries), who incidentally had quite a passion for Rugby, playing in the Edinburgh Wanderers as a young man. So no doubt he would have approved of its use at the 1990 match.

Search out both versions. The Corries gently singing it from the 1960s, played on a lute and bodhran drum in the crumbling ruins of a Scottish castle, and the defiant 1990s rendition from the Scottish rugby team at Murray Field. Both are thoroughly worth listening to.

DECEMBER

3 December: Niel Gow's Lament to his Second Wife

Composer: Niel Gow

"Niel Gow, 1727 – 1807. Violinist and Composer", that is the title of the portraiture painting of him by Sir Henry Raeburn which hangs in the Scottish National Portrait Gallery, Edinburgh. Together Niel and his son Nathaniel composed almost 600 strathspeys, jigs and reels. This lament is one of his most often played laments. It is, as the name suggests, a lament to Niel's second wife, to whom he was married for 30 years. By all accounts the Gow family were gentle, open and honest people. I personally think that this lament speaks to that gentle nature.

I will be mentioning Niel again on 10 December and on that occasion, I will reference a Canadian fiddle player Hanneke Cassel. Sticking with that Canadian theme and paying homage to the great musical legacy that the Gows bestowed on the Americas, I am going to recommend that you listen to another Canadian fiddle player to hear this lament be played. 'Laura Risk with Voices of Music' is the term that you want to search out. It is a rich arrangement of this beautiful lament, played in a glorious setting by some extremely talented and empathetic musicians.

9 December: Western Isles

Composer: Peat and Diesel

On 9 December 2019 the band Peat and Diesel (#peatlemania) won the Best Live Act in the Scots Trad Music Awards. If you take a listen to their song 'Western Isles' you will find out why. It is loud, shouty and fun and combines genres of folk, country and rock in such a brilliant upbeat way. 'Western Isles' is a real get up and get on with your day type of song. It is an unusual line up of 'rock' musicians too, with Calum 'Boydie' Macleod on guitar and vocals, Uilleam 'Uilly' Macleod on drums and Innes 'Innes' Scott on Accordion. Boydie, Uilly and Innes come from Stornoway the main town of the Western Isles and the capital of Lewis and Harris. Take a look at their official video for 'Western Isles' and you'll see plenty of rugged, windswept images of the place. But a warning though, when you first get on to that video, you might think that you've landed in the wrong place. Don't let the newscaster put you off watching further. This is definitely a band to keep watching.

10 December: Miss Drummond of Perth

Composer: Niel Gow

This tune by Niel Gow is one of a vast array of Scottish fiddle tunes that made its way over the Atlantic with all those Scots in the 18th and 19th Centuries and landed firmly and squarely into the American Scots/Irish Appalachian music as well as the Canadian Cape Breton music catalogues. The tunes were taken over by the Scots and the Irish from their home countries and adopted and adapted for their new homelands. If you would like to hear a Cape Breton styling of the tune check out the fiddle lesson by Hanneke Cassel. She describes how the styling of the Strathspey (which is what Miss Drummond of Perth is) got adapted from the more gentler Scottish Country Dance Strathspey into a more aggressive Cape Breton styling – "don't be afraid to really crash down on those strings" she says – which is quite an apt way of describing the Cape Breton style!

Niel Gow was pretty much the inventor of the Strathspey. He is certainly accredited with creating a new technique known as up-bowing. This puts emphasis on the upward strike of the bow and really highlights the point in a dance where your feet are off the floor, which in turn gives the music a real energy.

We have met the Gow family before. Niel and Nathaniel on 26 July, then Niel again on 3 December. Today I am remembering him again because a statue was erected for him on 10 December 2020 in his childhood home of Dunkeld, Perth and Kinross. Unfortunately the Niel Gow festival, which is normally held around 22 March, was cancelled in 2020 due to Covid, and the same thing happened to the opening of his statue in December. This is a real shame because it had taken 17 years of lobbying by fans for the statue to come about. The plan is to have a festival at some point in the future. No doubt there will be some Niel Gow music played – possibly even this uplifting Strathspey of Miss Drummond of Perth.

Julia Read

11 December: The Highland Brigade at Magersfontein

Composer: John MacLellan

Take a listen to 'The Highland Brigade at Magersfontein'. What do you think, how does it make you feel? In my opinion it is quite a jolly little tune. It is written in ¾, with 3 beats to the bar, like a waltz, so it has that natural lilt that any ¾ march has. As any pipe band member will tell you, marching along to a ¾ always puts a spring in your step and that is just what this tune does. It has a unique little run in it, unique in terms of the bagpiping repertoire anyway, it just makes me want to skip. Count your way in and you'll find a hint to the skipping motif at bar 7 with a run of 8 notes, alternating regular and dotted. Then in the second half of the tune, this skipping motif goes up a notch in timing at bars 12 and 13 where we hear a run of lilting dotted semi quavers. This pattern of dotted and regular notes is used throughout the tune and there is no use of a really common bagpiping motif, namely a short first note landing onto a longer second, what I like to call a ta-chium. It is this use of regular notes, alternating with drawn out lilting dotted notes, together with the absence of ta-chiums that gives this tune such a unique and uplifting sound. The uplifting nature of this composition, to me, symbolises what must only have been a beautiful soul of the man that wrote it, Pipe Major John MacLellan. He had a penchant for naming his tunes after the places he had fought in and this one was no exception.

'The Highland Brigade at Magersfontein' was composed by John MacLellan because of the battle at Magersfontein. Let us go back in time and place to 11th December 1899, and drop us into South Africa, 300 miles South West of Johannesberg into the flat lands of Magersfontein. The rainstorm of the preceeding night had abated and a scorching day lay ahead. The generals made the same mistakes they were to make in world war I, namely to send men into battle in closed formation to a barrage of bullets and heavy artillery. It is recorded that 700 men were killed in the first 7 minutes! Many of them from the Highland Brigade. Amongst the Highland Brigade, made up from regiments such as The Black Watch, The Gordon Highlanders, The Seaforth Highlanders and others, there was John MacLellan, playing his bagpipes into battle. It was a bloody battle by all accounts and if you want to read more about The Battle of Magersfontein by all means go ahead. But what I take from this is the spirit of John MacLellan. He must have had a sense of humour and certainly a strong faith to have written such an uplifting tune as 'The Highland Brigade at Magersfontein' after experiencing this blood bath. He most certainly was a man of deep service. Take this extract from a letter he wrote back to his brother a month later on 11th Jan 1900.

"It was a very hard fight, indeed, and the Highlanders lost very heavily. We fought for fifteen hours and a half in the burning sun without food or water, and the bullets flying about our heads put me in mind of a hailstorm. [...] I was knocked about the field several times playing "Highland Laddie" on the pipes to gather the Highlanders together - some of them being very much disheartened after the hot reception they had in the morning. The pipes seemed to cheer them up [...]"[18]

What a service to his fellow man! To be in the midst of that maelstom and yet to be thinking of others, of how to cheer them up, gather them together and boost their morale. I certainly take something of the spirit of John MacLellan away from that. On this day of 11th December, going forward, I will find my own version of Highland Laddie to uplift the people around me. A smile to a stranger, a phone call to a friend, a donation to the food bank. Feel free to join me.

Julia Read

14 December: Ae Fond Kiss

Composer: Words - Robert Burns

I think that I am allowed one more Burns song, he was so prolific a poet/song writer afterall that it is hard to not just create an entry for Burns every day of the year! For this entry I'm offering Burns' most performed love song, namely 'Ae Fond Kiss'. It is a song of love between two people who were not allowed to be in love, for she, Nancy (Mrs Agnes Maclehose), was married. Nancy and Burns formed a strong loving platonic friendship and on 14 December 1791 they had their last meeting. She sailed to Jamaica to be with her estranged husband and Nancy and Burns never met again. Burns wrote 'Ae Fond Kiss' as a farewell love poem and sent it to

Nancy on 27 December, just as she set sail. On the 14th December every year, Nancy wrote this in her diary ….

'this day I shall never forget, for this was the last day that I saw Robert'

She did this every year for 40 years, that is how enduring her love was.

There are many recordings of Ae Fond Kiss. I am going to recommend Robyn Stapleton. Robyn is a Scottish singer, from Dumfries and Galloway. She studied at the Royal Conservatoire of Scotland and in 2014 she won the BBC Radio Scotland Young Traditional Musician award. Her voice is so warm and rich. I hope that you enjoy this fabulous rendition.

21 December: Amazing Grace

Composer: Words - John Newton

There isn't much about Amazing Grace that is Scottish. It is based on a hymn tune called 'New Britain'; American composer William Walker was the man responsible for this. The words were penned by the English minister John Newton and reflects I believe the spiritual awakening that he went through in his journey from captain of a slave ship to Anglican minister. So, no there isn't much about it that is Scottish except that is, that every Scottish bagpiper in the world knows how to play it and will have played it so many times that they'll have lost count. As a bagpiper myself, I feel very confident in making this statement because it is often the first tune that is taught on the bagpipes. It is, to me, almost synonymous with the bagpipes. It has a powerfulness when played on the bagpipes, whether that is from a solo piper or a full pipe band. A format that pipe bands frequently use is for a solo piper to play the tune, then have the full band come in on the second verse which takes the listener from a poignant start to an incredibly powerful impactful finish; a dynamic that is very fitting to the truth behind the words. You will hear this demonstrated if you go to the Royal Edinburgh Military Tattoo.

I have placed Amazing Grace here on 21 December because it was the date of John Newton's death. That is not intended to be in anyway morose, but rather to reflect the spiritual awakening that he so obviously went through in his life. On 21 December 1807 John Newton passed away and went into the arms of his maker, leaving behind a hymn that is loved the world over.

25 December: Precious

Composer: Annie Lennox

Maybe you were given this book for Christmas and are now all settled down for the afternoon with your slice of Christmas cake and have opened this book up to today to see what it has to offer. If so, may I welcome you into this little gang of fellow readers who have spent the past year getting a little taste of Scotland each month through its music. I hope that you enjoy this entry and all the other entries that you will dip in and out of over the coming year.

Today we are going to Aberdeen, 130 miles north of Edinburgh, on the East coast of Scotland. 50 miles inland, to the West, is the Queen's summer estate of Balmoral, where every year on the first Sunday in September the Queen and her family attend the Braemar highland gathering. Stay in Aberdeen and experience the culture of the city, or head to the glorious beaches and have a chocolate slider[19], or head for a drive up the river Dee for a whisky tasting at the Lochnagar distillery. Whatever you do, today I'm going to recommend listening to Annie Lennox's 'Precious' from her 'Diva' album, because today is her birthday and she was born in Aberdeen.

The song 'Precious' is one of those songs that could be about quite a few things. Many people might think of their own child and how absolute love grew in their hearts with the arrival of their 'little angel'. Others might think of a lover as being their 'little angel'. For me I think of God and the peace filled path that I have been taken on through faith. Whatever 'Precious' says to you, I hope that you can put it on today and enjoy the beat of the music and the message of gratitude within it. Today certainly seems to be an appropriate day to acknowledge gratitude. So, here's to Aberdeen for giving the world Annie Lennox and here's to that 'little angel' that is in your life.

26 December: I Love a Lassie

Composer: Sir Harry Lauder

Take yourself off to Glasgow today. Before you were born, back to 26 December 1905. You are a wee laddie or wee lassie and your mam and dad are taking you and your kid sister off to see the pantomime Aladdin at the Theatre Royal, Glasgow. In a slight twist to the Aladdin story the wicked magician employs a young Glasgow boy as his apprentice, Roderick MacSwankey (played by Harry Lauder). There is lots of laughter, lots of 'oh no he isn't' and 'he's behind you'. As the standing ovation finishes your mam and dad bundle you out into the cold and you make your way along Hope Street to catch the tram home. You and your sister skip along singing the words to one of the songs from the Pantomime 'I Love a Lassie'. But it's not just you two kiddies that are singing it, your parents are humming it too. When you get to the tram stop, everyone else is doing the same. This song, that immediately landed in people's hearts, was such a huge hit for Lauder that it made him a worldwide star. Lauder wrote the song specifically for this Aladdin pantomime. Oh yes he did! (sorry).

Lauder wrote many other famous songs, including 'Roaming in the Gloaming' and 'Keep On Til the End of the Road', which according to Winston Churchill's body guard Churchill used to sing during WWII as a way to keep him going. Churchill described Lauder as Scotland's greatest ever ambassador. Prior to his efforts in WWII, Sir Harry Lauder had been knighted in 1919 for his incredible efforts to raise funds for the WWI war effort. He was noted as the highest paid performer in the world. Eight years after you and your sister saw him in the Aladdin pantomime, he was paid around £1,000 for just one single performance; this is back in 1913! You happened to see him right at the point that his career was about to jettison off into the stratosphere.

'I Love a Lassie' is still a well recognised song by most Scots. It has passed through the generations by being recorded by the likes of Andy Stewart, as well as its melody being used in a Scottish children's song 'I Love a Sausage'. It is a grand song and lucky you, you got to hear it first.

31 December: Let's Go Round Again

Composer: Average White Band

Hang that glitter ball up, put your dancing shoes on and get ready to party! We're off, one more trip around the sun coming up – Let's Go Round Again. Scottish funk R&B band, Average White Band, wrote the perfect song to get us on that dance floor and party the night away, so what are you waiting for. I won't hold you up by making you read a long history of the band from their emergence in Dundee in the 1960s through their various hits and travels to London and the States. You won't want to be staying in and reading on a night like tonight. It's New Years Eve. Are you ready?

As for me, I'm grabbing my bagpipes and heading off to my New Year's Eve gig. I'll see you on that dance floor at midnight for a rendition of Auld Lang Syne. Wishing you the very best for a happy, joy filled year ahead. Let's Go Round Again then shall we!

REFERENCES

[1] 16 children and 1 adult were killed in the Dunblane primary school when a lone gunman fired his weapons 109 times

[2] Glesga = colloquial for Glasgow

[3] 'The Search' was released on 1 June 1990.

[4] Attributed to Donald Cameron in 2005 book "Pipers," Dr. William Donaldson

[5] http://www.redstone-tech.com/gerry_bsb/folk_roots_1988.htm

[6] https://number1albums.com/city_to_city_-_gerry_rafferty_july_8_1978/

[7] The exact lyrics aren't being quoted for copyright reasons.

[8] A Rowie is a savoury bread roll made from flaky pastry. It is a bit like a flattened out savoury croissant. Delicious with butter and jam.

[9] The Glasgow Herald, 9 August 1912

[10] https://my.strathspey.org/u/anselm/stories/reelofthe51st/

[11] Robert passed away of a brain tumour and was buried in an unmarked grave in Eastlands Cemetery, Galashiels.

[12] Eastern United States Pipe Band Association

[13] The Ptarmigan was a rugged Wide Area Network used by the British Army, as such it was one component of a battlefield rugged mobile communications system. Initially operational in 1985, development for Ptarmigan started in 1973.

[14] Born Robert Coull Wellins 24 Jan 1936 and passed away 27 October 2016. He grew up in Gorbals, Glasgow and became a legend of the British Jazz Scene. He was part of the very famous album Jazz Suite Inspired by Dylan Thomas's "Under Milk Wood"

[15] 'Forest' in this sense doesn't necessarily refer to a wooded area as we know it, but rather in the sense of a Royal Forest from Tudor times. This Royal Forest was really a piece of land that was legally set aside, much like the way we refer to Reserves in modern day parlance.

[16] See 11th November for a fuller description of the Common Ridings.

[17] MG Alba Scots Trad Music Awards 2020

[18] https://www.angloboerwar.com/forum/17-memorials-and-monuments/29397-piper-john-mclellan-d-c-m-highland-light-infantry

[19] A chocolate slider is a local term that describes ice cream scoops sandwiched between two chocolate waifers. Delicious any time of the year,

even on Christmas day.

Printed in Great Britain
by Amazon